Grampy, Grampy and Grandma... What Did You Do When You Were Growing Up?

*The Lives of Two Kids
in the 1960s and 1970s*

Also by Chris Warnky

Grampy, Grampy and Grandma... What Did You Do When You Were Growing Up?

The Lives of Two Kids in the 1960s and 1970s

Chris Warnky

Columbus, Ohio

2025

Chris Warnky
1440 Mentor Drive
Westerville, Ohio 43081

Editor: Gwen Hoffnagle
Book Layout © 2017 BookDesignTemplates.com

Grampy, Grampy and Grandma… What Did You Do When You Were Growing Up?: The Lives of Two Kids in the 1960s and 1970s / Chris Warnky – 1st ed.
ISBN 979-8-9863178-6-1

Dedication

This book is dedicated to my grandchildren, Hannah, Lydia, and Grace. I hope this book gives you great insight into the lives of your grandparents, who have significantly influenced your parents. This book may help you understand some of the reasons your parents believe what they believe and do what they do. Grandma and I have so much to be thankful for because of our life experiences. I hope you can learn something from us through all we share in the pages ahead. *Grampy, Grampy and Grandma* is one way we hope to pass on our lives and legacy to you.

May you live a blessed and active life, just as we have into our late 60s.

Contents

Introduction

Once upon a time two grandchildren sat on a couch playing with their grandmother and grandpa. The grandpa was often called "Grampy," and frequently addressed as "Grampy, Grampy." The kids were laughing and playing with Grampy, who was known to come up with peculiar reasons to tickle each grandkid, either because of something they said or did, or to help fix a problem he had invented. The remedy was often a tickle under the chin, in an armpit, on the knees, or at a hip. They were always laughing, playing, and making up situations or stories about what was going on, usually ending in some version of tickling and laughing. Both girls loved to hear stories. No matter where they were or what they were doing, they loved making up stories, too. They especially enjoyed telling stories about or featuring their stuffed animals, which they called "stuffies," or their Legos.

The older girl, Hannah, about seven or eight at the time, turned to Grampy and asked, "Grampy, Grampy, what did you do when you were growing up?" Well, Grampy thought for a moment, putting his finger to his chin and tilting his head while he pondered the question. He responded with several exciting, true short stories centered on his escapades in the neighborhood storm sewers. Their eyes lit up as he described the experiences, so he continued sharing the sewer stories. These were large storm sewers, easy for any kid to bend over and walk through. The grandkids' parents also started paying very close attention to what Grampy was going to say to their kids. Grampy continued in detail, describing how a friend had his head stuck in a sewer opening, and then how he and his friends would explore more than a mile of the storm sewer pipes underneath the neighborhood. The grandkids and their parents continued to listen intently to

Grampy's stories for the next few minutes. When he stopped the grandkids begged to hear more. "Tell us more about the sewers." Their parents were a little concerned about what their kids were hearing, but it was all true. These were Grampy's childhood adventures, back in the 1960s, when he was just a little older than the grandkids were now.

* * *

This was the birth of the idea to capture Grampy's life experiences in a book, focusing on what I did as a kid.

Well, that concept took on a life of its own. As I began documenting my youth I also started thinking about my parents' lives. That birthed yet another idea. Why not add a section about my parents, starting with what they did as kids? As this idea mushroomed and I began documenting many of my parents' experiences, I realized it was going to be a much longer book than I had initially planned. So I decided to divide my *Grampy, Grampy* book into two books. As it turned out, I first published *Great Grampy and Grammy...: What Did You Do When You Were Growing Up?*, the second book in this planned set, a book about my parents' lives, and I hope you enjoy *Great Grampy and Grammy* as you learn about my parents. Through asking them about their childhoods, I also learned a lot more about my parents.

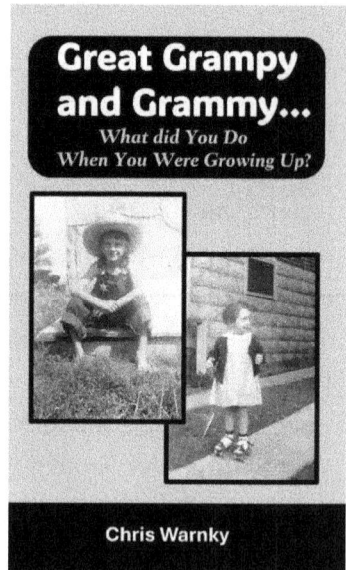

Great Grampy and Grammy...
What did You Do When You Were Growing Up?

Chris Warnky

Grampy, Grampy and Grandma... What Did You Do When You Were Growing Up?: The Lives of Two Kids in the 1960s and 1970s is about my life and a little about my wife, Carolyn's, life experiences. This book was initially written for my grandkids, but I believe that many of my other relatives will also find it quite interesting, including my sister, brother, and nieces and nephews. I also hope it's a fun and interesting quick read for those who have never met me or Carolyn, those who are in their 50s, 60s, and 70s and remember some of these experiences themselves, and those who are much younger and wonder what it was like to grow up in the 1960s and '70s.

We didn't often have cameras available to take photos when I was growing up, and photos that were taken were on film, prints, or slides. My dad had a nice single-lens reflex (SLR) camera that he used mostly during vacations. My mom didn't have a camera and I didn't receive my first camera until I was in late elementary school. We didn't have cell phones with cameras, so I don't have a lot of photos from my younger years, but throughout the book I share some of the photos that were taken to help you better appreciate the experiences that I share.

Here's a quick introduction to Carolyn and me. I was born in 1957, and Carolyn was born a little over a year later in 1958. We were married in June of 1979, so I was 22 and Carolyn was 21. We have two children: Timothy Eric Warnky was born on June 6th, 1982, and Michelle Marie Warnky was born almost two years later on June 4th, 1984.

A lot has changed since I was a child, but a lot remains the same. You will learn about our involvement in various interesting activities, some of which you may have participated in as a young kid and others you may not have even heard of. Some of these activities no longer exist, and some of the items in the stories are no longer used today. I hope my memories are both interesting and helpful to you as you move along this road of life.

Few people take the time to document their lives, and even fewer are open and transparent enough to share them with the world. Capturing and sharing these memories is my gift to you. To the best of my knowledge and my memory, these are the details of my childhood. I share many experiences that younger people today can no longer even dream of because they've gone out of sight and out of mind. Things have changed a lot, yet many of our experiences are probably the same.

This book is primarily about my youth, and in the last chapter Carolyn shares a little about the contrasts to hers. Let's delve into some fascinating stories from the past nearly 70 years.

Chapter 1

Grampy, Grampy: Chris Eric Warnky

I was born in 1957 to Russ and Carolyn Warnky in St. Louis, Missouri. I grew up in a great, loving family. My sister, Colleen, is two years younger than I, and my brother, Mark, is five years younger.

Since being born I have lived in eight decades, two centuries, and two millennia!

What We Didn't Have

To give you a sense of how life was different when I was growing up, when I was born we didn't have cell phones; dishwashers; microwave ovens; CDs; DVDs; word processors; personal computers; spreadsheets; email; the internet; tablets; digital photos; TV remote controls; DVRs; satellite; cable; streaming; ebooks; Facebook; TikTok; Instagram; Amazon; phone apps for checking the temperature, getting news, playing games, sharing photos, and sending messages; GPS and map programs in the car or on the phone; cruise control; seatbelts; cars that would go farther than 20 miles on a gallon of gas; *American Ninja Warrior*; or many of the fast-food options of today.

In many ways life was very different. All of these things were invented or came into being during my lifetime.

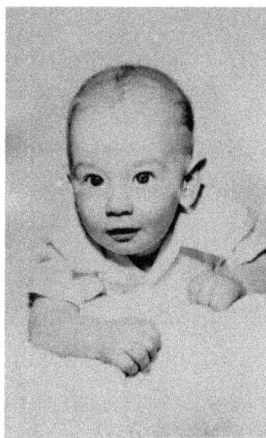

Chapter 2

Preschool and Kindergarten Years

The memories in this chapter are from after my family moved to Hennepin Drive in St. Louis in 1961. I don't remember much from before I was four years old. I didn't attend a preschool, but these are things I remember from my life before first grade from about 1961 through the spring of 1963, when I finished kindergarten.

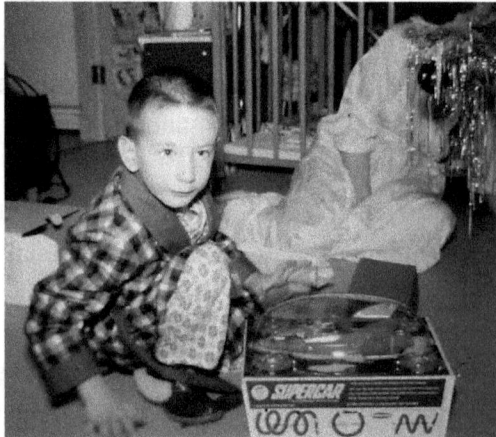

A Brick Hits Me on the Head

One of my earliest childhood memories is that of making a one-sided tent adjoining our high concrete back porch. I used a blanket for my tent, securing it in place with bricks on the top end and additional bricks on the ground to hold it down. I was moving around in this one-sided tent, and I must have accidentally bumped the blanket, which pulled one of the top bricks off the porch and down onto my head. I know it hurt, and I never again tried to make a one-sided tent. It was likely my first head injury – not too serious, but memorable – something to learn from.

My Toys

Tinker Toys

I enjoyed playing with Tinker Toys, colorful wooden sticks that slid into holes in round wooden wheels to build various structures.

Erector Set

Erector Sets were also for building creative structures. They consisted of thin metal strips lined with holes where screws and nuts were placed to hold the strips together. There were different kinds of sets available; mine included gears and a motor so you could create moving structures like a windmill or a Ferris wheel. They were sturdy, substantial structures that stood up to hours of playtime.

Mighty Matilda

This was a large toy aircraft carrier with small plastic jets that could be launched from the spring-loaded surface. It also had a working elevator run by batteries to move airplanes from the lower deck to the upper deck. This fun toy was over two feet long, with a blue base and a yellow top. I played with it for hours at a time.

Robot Commando

This was my first, and probably only, robot. It had a battery-controlled remote control at the end of a cable. This nearly two-foot-tall blue battle robot would roll forward and backward. It made a clicking sound as it moved forward. It had arms that could swing forward, hurling whatever was in its grasp, and a top that opened to reveal a missile it could shoot toward its target. It was the ultimate battle robot, designed to win a war against any enemy.

G.I. Joes

I enjoyed playing with my G.I. Joes and Illya Kuryakin (from *The Man from U.N.C.L.E.* TV show) dolls. They were the male versions of Barbies, for boys. I played army with them and also secret agents. I enjoyed making up stories and situations for them to live through. I was beginning to fall in love with basketball, so I also formed a basketball team with my five dolls. I called my team the Colorado New Generation.

Man from U.N.C.L.E. Guns

I fell in love with *The Man from U.N.C.L.E.*, a spy series. My friends and I would pretend to be various agents from the TV show. I received a *Man from U.N.C.L.E.* gun set as a gift, with multiple attachments and a holster, and the Illya Kuryakin doll I mentioned above. I played *Man from U.N.C.L.E.* for hours.

Cowboy Guns

From an early age I watched many TV shows featuring cowboys and spies. I was accustomed to seeing guns all the time. I received many toy guns and holsters as presents, primarily wild-west styles based on TV shows. My friends and I made believe we were various characters beating the bad guys or Indians.

Comic Books

I enjoyed the colorful *DC* comic books. Some of my favorite heroes were Green Lantern, Superman, Batman and Robin, Adam Strange, Aquaman, Wonder Woman, the Green Arrow, and The Flash. They were the Justice League. My friends and I would make believe we were these heroes and pretend we were fighting off the enemy.

Stagecoach Riding

Colleen and I used to play cowboys and cowgirls with our cowboy outfits, little toy guns, and holsters. We would climb up onto the narrow top shelf of an upright wooden toybox that our dad had made and pretend we were riding on a stagecoach and being attacked by thieves we had to shoot at. Carolyn and I still own that toybox. It's in the basement of our current home. It's over 60 years old, yet it still works well and now holds our excess groceries. It's been in our family for a very long time.

Basement Shows

Colleen and her best friend, Janet, used to love to dress up and put on shows for us in our basement. They would sing a song or dance to music. Colleen and Janet are still close today.

I Hit Jimmy with a Hammer

I used to play with Jimmy, the kid who lived across the street from us. We were good friends and we played together a lot. One day we were playing carpenter in his basement and we got into an argument. Unfortunately I had a tiny toy hammer in my hand. It had a wooden handle and a small metal head, only about three inches by a half inch, but it was still dangerous. I hit Jimmy on the head with my hammer and he started to cry. There was no blood, but it probably created a little bruise on the top of his head. I got into big trouble, and my parents took away my hammer. I was not able to play with it again for almost a year, until I was older and more responsible.

Jimmy and I were playing together again a year later, and again we got into an argument, and again... I hit Jimmy on the head with my hammer. I had not learned my lesson. That hammer was taken from me and was never seen again. I had hit him on the head twice. I had anger issues that I needed to deal with. I must have learned my lesson after this second time because I did not have anger or tantrum issues like that again. This was a traumatic experience for me, and I wonder what Jimmy remembers.

Dad Gets Stuck

One day I was walking down the sidewalk from our front door to our driveway. I heard a muddled voice, like it was coming from a cave. I listened a little more, and quickly realized it was my dad's voice, but I couldn't see him and couldn't understand what he was saying. As I moved closer to our carport, I could tell the sound was coming from that direction. I continued to listen and heard my dad calling, "Help! Get me out of here!" I soon discovered that he was in the trunk of our sedan. I wondered what was going on. I didn't have any keys, so I went back into the house to find my mom. She came to my dad's rescue, opening the trunk so he could get out. He had been working on something inside the trunk of the car, maybe a taillight or something like that, and the lid of the trunk accidentally closed on him, trapping him in the trunk. What a crazy experience for him, and a very surprising one for me as well.

Chapter 3

Grades One through Three

From the summer of 1963 through the spring of 1966, when I graduated from third grade, I was six through the first part of my ninth year.

The Lawn Maze

Sometimes my dad cut our lawn in a clever way that left curving, twisting paths that intersected, creating a maze-like area where we'd run around and play tag. It was an easy way to create a neat playground for us. I think he primarily did this in the backyard; it probably wouldn't have looked very nice for our neighbors in the front yard.

Weed Guns

We used to pull out of the ground a very tall weed that had a seed-head on it, bend and turn the stem around the portion of the stem just below the head, and then pull on the middle of the stem to shoot the head off of the weed so it would fly forward, usually at each other. It was a safe way to play and have fun shooting each other with little fluffy weeds.

Our Swimming Pool

In the back corner of our backyard we had a green metal swing set that we would climb and play on, and only a few feet away was a large, round, metal feeding trough that we used as a swimming pool.

It was about eight feet in diameter and about three feet high. During those many really hot, 100-degree and nearly-100-degree days we would put on our suits and head with our friends to our swimming pool. When we weren't using it we covered it with overlapping wavy metal sheets – about four of them – to keep bugs and leaves out of the water. There was no chlorine; it was just normal faucet water. I don't remember ever going to a large public in-ground pool until I was in one of my last years of high school.

My parents had a garden for a few years. I seem to remember planting pumpkins and watermelon. I don't remember much more than that. I sure didn't have a gardening heritage from my parents.

The Clothes Chute

Our house on Hennepin Drive had a clothes chute in the main hallway. It was a tin chute, about one foot by six inches, facing downward into the basement, about four feet long. It had a spring-loaded door that would remain closed unless you pulled it down and out to open it. It was used to send dirty clothes down to the basement to be washed without having to carry them down. At some point my dad installed a buzzer on the inside of the chute so that someone in the basement could be informed that something was going on, like lunch or dinner time, or time to leave for the store or church. It was also a handy way to have a conversation from upstairs to downstairs, or vice versa. This was beneficial years later when my dad built a bedroom downstairs for me to live in.

I Hit Jimmy on the Head Again

Jimmy and I remained good friends, and one day we were playing in the basement at my house. Jimmy went to use the bathroom my dad had built in the basement, and I got the crazy idea that I would take the wooden base off a little flagpole we had in the basement and act like I was going to toss it at him like you would a frisbee. It was a thin piece of wood about four inches by six inches and about a half-inch thick, just big enough to support a three-foot-tall pole holding a five-by-eight-inch Christian flag. I wound up like I was going to throw a frisbee, and as he walked out of the bathroom I started to fling my arm and wrist forward. Somehow the base slipped out of my fingers, went hurling toward Jimmy, and landed with a sharp, spinning edge right on his forehead, causing a cut a few inches long. It immediately started to bleed, and as the blood flowed down his forehead I thought for sure I had killed my best friend. It was supposed to be a joke. It wasn't supposed to come out of my hand. It wasn't supposed to hit him at all, let alone in the head. I was so sorry, and I immediately and repeatedly blurted it out, hoping it would all go away. I only remember my side of the story. I think my parents put a cold washcloth up to his forehead and stopped the bleeding. He didn't have to be taken to the hospital or to the doctor, but I sure remember the regret I felt when I accidentally let go of that piece of wood. I was so sorry and am still today.

Practical jokes need to be safe and not dangerous. I made a terrible choice, and again, Jimmy paid the price.

Jimmy and his family eventually moved to a different neighborhood – not because of me, but we lost touch aside from crossing paths a few times in high school. He was a great baseball pitcher who developed his skills through hours of work with his dad.

Getting Spanked

When we misbehaved, my siblings and I were spanked across our butts by hand, with a paddle, or with a belt. I definitely remember times when my mom would say, "I'm going to go get the paddle!" It was a rounded, wooden paddle, the kind that used to have a rubber band and ball attached, which was a game in which you tried to repeatedly tap the ball with the paddle each time the rubber band pulled it back toward the paddle. I didn't look at it as a game, but rather as a spanking tool that I didn't want used on me. If I did something my mom felt was really wrong, she would say, "Dad is going to give you the belt when he gets home!" And he did. I definitely remember being spanked, and it hurt, but not for long. I only remember being spanked in grade school, and maybe when I was younger. It sure helped me respect my parents' authority. They spanked us because they believed they were directed to do so by the Bible verse Proverbs 13:24: "Whoever spares the rod hates his son, but he who loves him is diligent to discipline him."

Carolyn and I also spanked Tim and Michelle when they were disobedient. We spanked when they were very young – rarely, with a warning in advance, and not in anger. I would tell the kids that if I told them I was going to spank them if they did something we said not to do, and they did it, I would be lying to them if I didn't follow through. Our kids were very well behaved and didn't need to be spanked very often, even when they were very young. We are so thankful for the many, many good choices they made as kids and the good decisions they continue to make as adults. I don't know if any

15

parents spank their kids these days. Surely there are some somewhere. Each set of parents has to decide what they feel is best for their kids.

A Lot of TV

Television was a big deal in my childhood. I watched a lot of it, from before I was old enough to go to school all the way through high school. Due to studies and other activities, my TV-watching dropped off considerably when I went away to college.

I don't remember all the shows, but over 90 shows I enjoyed are listed below so you'll get a good sense of the types of shows I watched. Most of them were 30 minutes long. We had a black-and-white television for years, even after shows began to be shown in color in the '60s, so I saw them in black and white.

My First Shows

When I was very young some of my favorite shows included *Commando Cody: Sky Marshal of the Universe,* and the *Adventures of Superman* TV series starring George Reeves, which was in black and white, transitioning to color in its later episodes. I would watch the show, then play Superman with my friends. I enjoyed watching the superheroes fly, break through walls, and take down bad guys. I watched *Batman* and *The Green Hornet* too.

I also enjoyed these black-and-white shows when I was very young: *Our Gang, The Little Rascals, The Three Stooges, Tarzan, Jungle Jim, The New Adventures of Charlie Chan,* and *Hercules* movies.

With Mom at Night

I remember watching many shows at night with my mom, often while my dad was either studying or off at his evening college classes. I enjoyed watching *The Untouchables*, about gangsters and the police; and *Combat!*, about World War II U.S. soldiers fighting the Germans. Both shows included a lot of violence – not gory, but a lot of shooting and killing. We also watched *Route 66, Highway Patrol, Dragnet, The Andy Griffith Show, The Real McCoys,* and *The Many Loves of Doby Gillis.*

With Mom during the Day

In the afternoons, when I returned from school, I watched some soap operas with my mom. I especially remember *One Life to Live.*

Saturday Morning Cartoons

I also watched cartoons early on Saturday mornings. My favorite show initially was *Mighty Mouse*. I also watched *The Yogi Bear Show, Felix the Cat, Space Ghost, Thunderbirds, Dick Tracy, Mister Magoo,* and *The Adventures of Rocky and Bullwinkle.*

Before School

I often watched TV while eating breakfast and waiting for my bus to arrive. I watched *Fury, The Range Rider, The Lone Ranger, My Friend Flicka, Sky King,* and *The Roy Rogers Show.*

In the Evenings

I watched a lot of black-and-white Westerns including *The Rifleman, Lawman, Gunsmoke, Have Gun – Will Travel, The Rebel, Wagon Train, The Legend of Jesse James,* and *The Wild Wild West.* I played hours and hours of cowboys with my friends.

Family Shows

I also watched a lot of family-relationship shows with my mom. We watched *My Three Sons, Father Knows Best, The Adventures of Ozzie and Harriet, The Bob Cummings Show, The Patty Duke Show,*

Dennis the Menace, Hazel, Leave It to Beaver, The Dick Van Dyke Show, I Love Lucy, Flipper, The Donna Reed Show, and *Family Affair.*

Variety Shows

We also watched *The Carol Burnett Show, The Red Skelton Show,* and, when I was in grade school, *Rowan & Martin's Laugh-In.*

As a Family

As a family we watched *Bewitched, I Dream of Jeannie, Mission: Impossible,* and the British secret agent show *The Avengers.* In my later high school years we also watched *The Love Boat* and *Love, American Style.*

My Personal Favorites

As I moved into my teens some of my personal favorites were shows about secret agents, spies, detectives, and police. I enjoyed *I Spy, T.H.E. Cat, Honey West, The Man from U.N.C.L.E., It Takes a Thief, Perry Mason, The MOD Squad, The Rat Patrol, Garrison's Gorillas, The Fugitive, Charlie's Angels,* and *Adam-12.*

Comedies

I watched comedies including *The Flintstones, The Beverly Hillbillies, The Addams Family, The Munsters, F Troop, McHale's Navy, Gilligan's Island, The Monkees,* and, later in high school, *Happy Days* and *Fantasy Island.*

Mysteries and Adventures

I watched *The Outer Limits, The Twilight Zone,* and *The Alfred Hitchcock Hour,* and especially liked adventures like *Sea Hunt, Lost in Space,* and *Voyage to the Bottom of the Sea.*

Sports

I can't leave out sports. I also watched a good deal of St. Louis Cardinals baseball, some St. Louis and then Atlanta Hawks basketball, a little St. Louis Cardinals football, some St. Louis Blues hockey, and some professional and college basketball games.

It's interesting that we didn't watch the news. And I was always in bed before the nighttime talk shows like *The Tonight Show*, so I didn't see any of them. I didn't read many books during these years. My time was spent playing and watching TV.

Roller Derby

Collen, Mark, and I would watch roller derby competitions on TV in which teams raced and chased each other around a wooden, banked, oval racetrack. Then we would head to the basement and race around our ping-pong table, imitating our heroes like Big Bad Bob Woodbury. It was so much fun to grab the leg at a corner of the ping-pong table and sling myself forward with even more power and speed than I had coming into the corner.

Devotions

Most nights after dinner my family participated in what we called Devotions. During this time we would sing a chorus or two, read a devotional passage and some scripture, and then pray together. This would often take 10 to 15 minutes, and frequently it was while our friends from the neighborhood were out in our front yard playing and waiting for we kids to be done. I'm sure this was a good investment in our spiritual lives, but at the time it was a real pain to know that on many evenings our friends were just outside waiting on us.

The Party Line

We had party-line phone service while I was growing up. That means we shared our phone line with others. When we picked up the corded handset from the phone on the wall to call someone, we sometimes heard someone already on the line. We would apologize and coordinate with them to learn when they would be done and off the line so we could use it. We didn't know the people we shared the line with; they weren't local neighbors. This was life at that time. I still have that phone number memorized: HA9-3947, or Harrison 9-3947. We didn't use an area code, and the first two digits were letters, short for the local community, like Harrison in our case. We had a party line for quite a few years.

Skittles

We used to play skittles in our basement. We had a skittles table that my Grandpa Warnky built probably before I was born. It was played on a two-and-a-half-by-four-foot table with walls all around the outside, using a spinning top, which was a peg with a wheel-shaped head. You wound the top with a string, stuck it through a hole at the end of the table, and then pulled the string hard to create a powerful spin. The top would spin for up to a minute or more through a maze of three rooms at the front of the game, spinning through some of its doors and then into the large middle section where there were pins to be knocked down. Each pin that was knocked down by the spinning top counted as a point for the person who spun it. At the back end of the table were three more little rooms, as at the front. If the top went in there and knocked down pins in those rooms, you would earn even more points per pin. Sometimes a player would pull the string so hard that it would jolt the whole table, knocking down all the pins, and we would have to set them all up again. It was a fun game. We would rotate who spun the top and see who earned the most points from their spin.

My Cinnamon Toast

One morning my dad was helping me with my breakfast and he accidentally put chili powder on what was supposed to be cinnamon-and-sugar toast. A piece of pretoasted bread was supposed to be buttered, then lightly sugared, and then sprinkled with cinnamon on top. It was then rebroiled to help the sugar and cinnamon sizzle with the butter. When I took my first bite, I quickly learned something was really wrong. I realized that he had accidentally put chili powder on the toast instead of cinnamon. I still remember that mistake over 60 years later. It must have tasted terrible.

Searching for Christmas Presents

I was a very obedient child. I generally did whatever my parents told me to do. At Christmastime I would search the entire house looking for the presents we would open on Christmas day. I didn't know whether they would be wrapped or unwrapped, but I was convinced they were somewhere in the house. I looked through every room, every cabinet, and every closet, except for the workroom in the basement where my parents told us not to go during certain times of the year. This was where the washing machine and dryer were, and my dad's tools and workbench. I never even thought of looking there because my parents said the room was off limits. A few years down the road I finally caught on: That's where they kept the Christmas presents until they were wrapped and ready for display under the Christmas tree. I was a trusting child and never even considered going into that room.

"Turn Tight!"

I loved riding in the car with my Uncle Gary. Anytime we would come to a turn on the road we would all call out, "Turn tight!" and he would sharply turn the steering wheel so that we would be thrust to the left or right in our seats. This was well before we had seat belts in cars, so we would slide from one side of the vehicle to the other each time he made a turn. It was a blast for us and a memorable experience. I continued this tradition with my kids at times, and I think they also really enjoyed these antics.

The Gun in the Bathroom

One night I woke up in the middle of the night and needed to go to the bathroom; I had eaten a great deal of watermelon that evening before going to bed. I rose from my bed and quietly walked to our bathroom, just one door to the right of my room. I was standing at the toilet peeing when I heard a sound to my left and saw the barrel of a handgun sticking through the blinds, aimed directly at my head, which nearly scared me to death. My heart was pounding and I immediately sprinted out of the bathroom and bounded into my mom and dad's bedroom, just across the hall from the bathroom, and leaped high and directly into their bed, screaming at the top of my lungs. I was so scared! While my mom hugged me tightly, my dad headed to the bathroom to see what was going on. There was a screen on the window, so there was no way that a gun could have been pointed at my head through the window and blinds. I had made up the whole story, likely based on the sound of the wind blowing through the open window, moving the blinds forward and backward, which made a bumping sound against the screen. I learned through that experience how powerful our minds are when we interpret what we hear or see; we can create stories that are not the reality of our situation or environment. I will always remember my scare that night from something that never actually happened.

Neighborhood Friends

There were a lot of kids in our neighborhood, which was almost a mile long – seven long parallel streets. After Jimmy moved away I had five other close friends who lived within three houses' distance from our house. My best friend was Bob, who lived almost directly behind us, and our backyards just touched. We played a lot together from at least first grade through fifth grade. Bob was a year older than I was, so he developed more extended friends and relationships earlier than I did, and with others in his grade as we moved further through our schooling. I haven't had much contact with Bob since I went to college, though I have seen him a few times and really enjoyed catching up with him.

Just up the street lived brothers Ray and Tommy. I played with them a lot as well. Ray was in Bob's grade, a year older than I, and Tom was a year younger, so none of these friends were in my grade or classes.

I also played with two kids who lived two doors down on the other side of our house, Marty and Terry. Marty was my age and Terry was a few years younger. In some ways they weren't really part of our inner circle, outcast in many situations. I was still friendly with them, but they took the brunt of many jokes and pranks over the years. I was kind of the intermediary between them and my other three friends. We played a lot of football and whiffle ball in Marty and Terry's backyard.

This was my closest gang. Many other kids I played with – at least 10 – lived streets away, so it was usually sports that brought all of us together.

Sledding

During our snowy winters many of my neighborhood friends and I would sled down the big hill just behind the houses across the street. We carried our sleds and climbed the 20- to 30-foot hill to slide down into the backyards of the Graineys and the Gordens. Both of those families had young kids, so it was acceptable to sled into their yards with them. The kids in those families were several years younger than we were, but their parents allowed us to play there. We spent many hours on those snowy hills without needing our parents to be involved or to drive us somewhere to sled. I remember having so much fun sledding down that hill in so many different ways – sitting upright, lying forward, and even standing up holding on to the rope attached to the front, trying to steer the sled down and not fall off. I know I fell many times, but it was so much fun.

Exploring the Neighborhood

We spent hours in the new neighborhood next to ours, just down the street, exploring the homes under construction. On days when no one was working there we were free to get in and climb all through and over the concrete and cement-block foundations and in and out of the wood-framed structures that had been built. We would climb into the upstairs and down into the basements of the shells of these new houses, exploring and having a blast. We didn't get hurt, but the potential was there. With the unfinished condition of the houses – no railings, exposed nails, and mounds of dirt – we sure could have been injured. But again, this was life back then; exploring and roaming through such places probably isn't possible for kids today.

Sleep-Outs

My friends and I – often Bob, Ray, and Tommy – would sleep in the backyard overnight in a tent or just in our sleeping bags. This allowed us to spend more time together playing, laughing, telling stories, and roaming the neighborhood. We sneaked around the nearby two or three blocks, hiding from cars, running around through backyards, and snooping around. Very few homes had fences, so we could roam from house to house around the block without restriction.

One night we skinny-dipped in Bob's neighbor's pool, trying to be very quiet. It felt so dangerous and exciting. The dad of that house was a police officer, which made it even more risky. We didn't get caught.

Another night, a little past midnight, we lifted a sewer lid off a concrete sewer platform next to the street – it was a large, heavy iron cover about 20 inches in diameter and about an inch thick – set it on its edge, slowly rolled it up to the top of the street, and let it roll down the street past several houses between us and the bottom of the street. It was loud as it rolled down the concrete street and into someone's yard. Looking back, that was really dumb. If a car had come up that street it could have been significantly damaged, and it could have hit a house or an outdoor decoration. It would have surely wiped out a mailbox. We were just kids thinking of playing, not the dangers of our fun. I am so thankful now that no one was hurt and nothing was damaged.

The Monkey Bars

One of my favorite school recess memories was playing on the monkey bars at Mount Pleasant Elementary School. I also played some softball and chased friends all across the asphalt playground and the grassy hills around our school. We had a large metal slide, a merry-go-round, painted lines on the pavement for certain games, and several other pieces of playground equipment, but the monkey bars (and jungle gyms) were my favorites. Our schoolyard had two sets of monkey bars, one at each end, with about five eight-foot-long bars mounted between them. We climbed across all of them from both below and above. We swung across them, tried standing on them, and pulled off all sorts of other stunts. We played a lot of tag, especially on the monkey bars. And the seven-foot drop was directly onto hard asphalt. I skinned my knees and elbows a lot and had some bloody scrapes from all of my falls – so much fun.

I remember one day during the Presidential Fitness Test, which all the kids had to take, I completed 19 pull-ups on one of those monkey bars. It was a lot more than most of the kids in my class. I was proud of my achievement. And I still love the monkey bars today. Each time I go into a ninja gym I'm reminded of my recess time out playing on the monkey bars.

A Reindeer

One year when I was in early grade school I played the part of a reindeer in our Christmas play at Mount Pleasant. It was probably my first experience being part of a live presentation to an audience. It was a big deal for me at the time, but I didn't even have a speaking, dancing, or individual singing role. I think I mainly had to walk onto the stage at the right time and stand there. I may have had to join in with the others in singing a Christmas carol.

Shocking and Sad Political News

I still have powerful memories of being in grade school and hearing about the assassinations of key government officials, including President John F. Kennedy (JFK) in November of 1963, when I was six years old and in about my third month of first grade, in Mrs. Domino's class. They rolled in a black-and-white TV so we could hear the news live during class. A few years later I learned about the killing of political leader Martin Luther King in April of 1968, when I was 11 and in fifth grade; and then later that next June, the brother of JFK,

Robert F. Kennedy (RFK), who was running for president. As a grade-schooler it was shocking to hear of these events. I remember hearing about the death of RFK while I was playing on the spinning wheel on our school playground. At that age I was sad, but didn't fully understand what was going on. This was a tough time for our nation.

The New York Subway

I remember my 1964 New York subway experience when, at around the age of seven, I almost got lost on a train that travels underground from one part of the massive city to another. I was there with my dad, my sister, my grandparents, and my aunt and uncle. It was a family trip and my mom was back at the hotel watching my brother, who was sick. We all stepped onto the subway and squeezed in with all the other passengers. Then one of my family members realized that we were on the wrong subway, so they all got off, but I was accidentally left behind. As the subway doors were closing, my uncle Rick reached out and held the two doors open as they were closing from each side, and I quickly squeezed through. He then let the doors close behind me. If he hadn't stopped those doors, I would have been riding to the next station all by myself in the heart of New York City. I have no idea how they would have found me or what I would have done – gotten off at the next station or just continued riding the train, waiting for them to come and get me.

Beatles Cards

When I was seven, in 1964, the Beatles, from Britain, had just become a big hit in the United States. It seemed everything was all about the Beatles. They even sold Beatles cards, like baseball cards. Just across the street from Mount Pleasant Elementary School there was a tiny store where students shopped during recess. They sold a variety of candies, including Pixie Stiks straws that contained sugar-sweet granules in various colors; little sugar beads stuck to two-inch-by-three-foot strips of paper, about three beads across; gum; other types of candy; baseball cards; and, of course, Beatles cards. I remember my friends and I buying Beatles cards several times.

The St. Louis Arch Time Capsule

In 1965, in my second-grade class, we each wrote our names on a piece of paper that was included in a time capsule placed in the topmost wedge of the St. Louis Arch as it was being completed. In some future year, when the time capsule is opened, my name will be one of the names people see. That is kind of fun to think about. My signature is already 60 years old. I hope I wrote legibly enough for future generations to read my name.

"Target Top"

Starting in about the fourth grade, my best friend nicknamed me "Target Top" because I often wore a knit stocking cap with colored rings – red, white, and black – with a black tassel on top. When he saw me coming up the stairs at school, looking down from the second floor, the top of my hat looked like a target. I'm not sure if I liked that name, but it stuck for a little while.

The 66 Club

I was an official member of The 66 Club at church. That meant that I was able to recite in order all 66 books of the Bible. I memorized them and could say them so fast that you could hardly understand all the names as I spoke them. I can still recite a string of many of them today, 60 years later. And I still have the formal certificate I received back in grade school.

Sword Drills

"Sword drills" were conducted at our church during Sunday School, during Training Union on Sunday nights, and during Royal

Ambassador meetings on Wednesday nights. A number of my church friends and I stood with our Bibles in our left hands, a leader would call out a Bible verse, and as soon as we heard the verse we had to quickly pull our Bible up and thumb through it to find that verse, putting our finger on it, and then step forward to reveal that we had found it. The goal was to be the first one to get there and win the competition. I won some of our sword drills. With practice we all became pretty quick at finding verses throughout the Bible.

Vacation Bible School

My family was very active in our church's Vacation Bible School (VBS). Our church was five miles from our house. My mom taught classes, and we invited the kids from our neighborhood to the VBS program. A number of them joined us, and my mom would drive all of us to the church. It was held during the day for one full week during the summer. We would decorate our car and drive in a parade with others from the church through the neighborhood to VBS. It was a big event for our church and for us.

Floating Boats

Immediately after a heavy rain, my friends and I enjoyed folding and then floating handmade paper boats down the gutter of our street. We would see how far we could get them to float before they stopped.

Snake on a Stringer

I joined my parents for a Labor Day camping weekend at Washington State Park, just a little south of St. Louis. Many family members had come for the weekend. My cousin Roddy had some fishing gear and was helping me catch fish in the river near our campsite. I hadn't fished much, so he shared his bamboo-stick fishing pole with me, and I caught about five bluegill. He had a stringer – a chain with hooks – and put each fish on a hook by its gills so that multiple fish could be held on a single chain. The stringer was then dropped into the water so the fish would stay alive and remain fresh if you wanted to scale and cook them later.

I was so proud of the fish that I had caught. As additional family members arrived at the campsite, I called out to them to see the fish. I would pull up the stringer and proudly show them. When my Aunt Jane arrived, I did the same thing; I called out to her and ran to the water to pull up my stringer and show her. But the look on her face really surprised me. She pointed in shock at the stringer I was holding up behind me, so I turned to look and I discovered that a snake had swallowed three of the fish – you could see them in its belly! – and its mouth was already halfway around the fourth one. My eyes lit up and I immediately dropped the stringer into the water. My cousin Roddy quickly ran and grabbed his BB gun and repeatedly shot the snake to kill it. I was so shocked by the experience that I don't remember what happened next, but it sure scared me. I haven't fished much since. I remember that scary experience. I'm sure I was never in danger, but it definitely surprised me.

Chapter 4

Grades Four through Six

This chapter is about my memories from the summer of 1966 through the spring of 1969, when I graduated from sixth grade. This is when I was nine through the first part of my turning 12.

Washing and Drying the Dishes

After dinner most nights, Colleen and I were in charge of washing the dishes we had used for the meal and then drying them with a towel. We alternated who did the washing and who would dry. Just outside our front or back door, our neighborhood friends were waiting for us to finish so we could come out and play. Doing the dishes felt like a real pain while our friends were playing just outside.

Getting to School

My grade school was about a mile away, and it took about 15 minutes to walk there. I sometimes rode the bus, but I walked or rode my bike to school a lot. I don't remember being driven by my parents. It was always me getting there on my own or with my friends.

Reading

I was, sadly, a very slow reader. I didn't read at home, and I didn't often see anyone else reading there either – not my parents, my brother, or my sister. In contrast, my good friend Bob enjoyed reading and read a lot – comic books and other books. Because I read so slowly and poorly, I often guessed at the answers to multiple-choice quizzes and tests in school. In many cases I didn't even read the questions or the answer options; when others started walking to the front to turn in their papers at the teacher's desk, I just stopped trying to read and quickly selected answers that looked random, like A, A, D, B, C, C, and A, and finished the quiz. I feared being the last one and being seen as a poor student.

I was a poor student. I just hoped to get enough answers correct to pass the quizzes and tests and, eventually, my grade. Had I actually taken the time to read and answer all the questions I would probably have been one of the last people to complete these assignments, and I would have gotten a lot more help from my teachers, becoming a better student. But I unfortunately chose what I thought was the easy way out. I didn't become a good student until my senior year in college, or maybe even later, once I started really caring about my development and personal growth in my 50s.

My poor reading skills have impacted me significantly for much of my life. In my 40s I took an audio-based speed-reading course that radically improved my reading skills, both speed and comprehension. It changed my life. I hope my younger readers have a much better start in life than I did, free from the fears and poor choices that drove me. I sincerely hope you work hard in school and get help when you need it. Getting help will benefit you for the rest of your life.

As a brief word of encouragement, despite my poor start in reading and education I have lived a very productive and successful life and have written and self-published 13 books. I have significantly expanded my knowledge, improved my writing, and acquired publishing skills. I've learned to lean heavily on experts and my own research to help me improve the final product of my writing, including my recent purchase and use of the Grammarly software program, and the tremendous value that my professional editor has provided to help clean up and polish my thoughts and feelings as I share them in book form.

Writing Sentences during Recess

In addition to not reading well, I also didn't pay attention in class. Before I received my glasses in third grade, I had trouble seeing what was written on the chalkboard. I talked a lot to my friends during class. Yes, I whispered, but I distracted my classmates and my teachers nonetheless. One of my teachers, Mr. Robison, who was a good teacher, dealt with people like me by having us write sentences during recess. I loved recess – the chance to go out and play – and he knew that. When I was caught talking I would get my name written up on the chalkboard and have to write a certain number of sentences during recess.

I was also a slow writer. I never worked on my writing skills, so I was slow and sloppy with my letters. The first time I was caught misbehaving in a particular week, I was assigned to write 15 sentences while the other kids played. I might be able to complete this assignment just before our 15-minute recess was over, so I would get to go out and play for a couple of minutes at the end. Then, if I were caught again that week, or again and again, the number of assigned sentences would be increased to 25 or 35 or more. Some of these penalties would take me more than one recess to complete. It doesn't seem I learned my lesson, because I kept getting caught and would again miss recess to write my sentences. I wrote the sentence below plenty of times, enough that I still remember it at age 68; it is permanently carved into my brain:

Although I have been warned many times not to talk in class, I have failed to listen to this warning, and I will therefore write this sentence 25 times.

Cardinals Baseball

In St. Louis we loved our Cardinals baseball team. I often listened to games being announced on KMOX 1120, and I watched some games on TV, especially during the years the Cardinals competed in the World Series. We even watched live World Series games during school on a black-and-white TV that sat on a rolling cart in our classroom. I experienced that in 1964, 1967, and 1968, during my first-, fourth-, and fifth-grade years. Those were special times. The whole city rallied around the Cardinals, wearing Cardinal clothing, talking about the Cardinals everywhere, and listening and watching every pitch of every game.

My favorite players and heroes during that time were Bill White, Bob Gibson, Steve Carlton, Lou Brock, Julian Javier, Dal Maxville, and Curt Flood. This is a special memory.

The Monkees

When I was nine, in 1966, the new TV show and singing group The Monkees came out. They were a big hit. They had their own sound and were somewhat a knockoff of the Beatles, except they started in the U.S., not England. Bob and I really enjoyed the Monkees, and we would put on a record and act like we were the band, singing along. Bob's favorite Monkee was Michael Nesmith and mine was Micky Dolenz, the drummer.

St. Louis Hawks and Basketball

When I was nine, in fourth grade, I came across the St. Louis Hawks basketball team; it may have been on TV or on the radio. After discovering them I fell totally in love with basketball, even more so than with our city's favorite sport, Cardinals baseball. I started listening to many of the Hawks' games on KMOX, with sportscaster Skip Caray. Skip was the son of the famous baseball announcer Harry

Caray, who announced Cardinals games with sportscaster Jack Buck. Harry eventually moved to Chicago and announced for the Chicago Cubs, our Cardinals' arch rival.

I loved the sound of Skip Caray's voice and his description of the game. It was then that I decided I wanted to be a professional sportscaster like Skip Caray. I even practiced announcing games I watched or attended, including our local pickup games and basketball games at our high school gym. I would even practice from the stands at professional games years later, watching the Spirits of St. Louis basketball team, sitting off by myself in isolated seats at their minimally attended games. I wanted to be Skip Caray. I even went to college focused on earning a degree in radio broadcasting, and I did so in 1979, about 10 years later. Although I never professionally announced a sporting event, I announced several basketball, football, and baseball games over the radio for my college teams.

One year, probably when I was in fifth grade, my parents took me to a live St. Louis Hawks basketball game. I got to see them in person. I felt like I had died and gone to heaven. It was a double event, which also featured the world-famous Harlem Globetrotters. I also enjoyed their crazy antics, but the Hawks were the main event for me.

I was shocked and very disappointed when I learned that the Hawks were being moved to Atlanta for the 1968 season. I was losing my favorite team. I didn't totally lose them; I kept listening to Skip Caray for years on my little transistor radio, sometimes under the covers in my bed when I was supposed to be sleeping. He moved with the team to Atlanta and continued to announce Atlanta Hawks basketball games. The Hawks, love of my heart, had left St. Louis, but I stayed a strong Hawks fan for many years.

Having fallen in love with basketball, I worked with my dad to install a four-inch-by-four-inch, fifteen-foot-high post in the backyard, then we cut and installed a large four-foot-by-four-foot plywood backboard, and painted it white. I added a nice one-foot-diameter blue Atlanta Hawks logo on the top portion. I spent hours and hours playing basketball in my backyard and anywhere else I could find. Basketball was my favorite sport among the ones I loved to play.

Becoming a Christian

Being raised in a strongly Baptist, Christian home, Colleen and Mark and I attended church each Sunday with our parents pretty much from the day we were born. Our Sunday routine included attending Sunday School, then the full church service, followed by Training Union in the evening, and then the evening church service. We also went to church on Wednesday nights, where I attended the Royal Ambassadors Program, followed by the church-wide prayer meeting. I received a lot of Christian teaching both at home and at church. At the age of nine, when I was in third grade, I asked Jesus to forgive my sins, and I became a Christian. I prayed with the pastor and then formally became a member of our Baptist church, coming to the front of the auditorium at the end of a service to proclaim my decision and commitment to the whole church body. Soon after that I was baptised during a service in front of our entire congregation.

New Testaments

I remember in 1966, when I was nine years old, my dad buying and then giving away or selling a hundred or more white-covered paperback New Testaments titled *Good News for Modern Man*. He believed it was a great, relatable version of the New Testament, and he wanted to get it into the hands of as many people as possible to encourage them to turn to God and change their lives.

Grandma Warnky

My Grandma Warnky died of lung cancer just before I turned nine. My grandfather found her lying on the bathroom floor. She was a heavy smoker. That was a real shock to all of us. She was only 55 years old, way too young to die. My dad was only 33 at the time.

A Trip with My Grandpa

I remember one distinct trip away from home for about a week without my parents. My Grandpa Warnky's wife had died, and he was alone, so he took me with him on a trip to Colorado. It was so much fun to be out and on my own with just my grandpa. This may have been when I fell in love with Colorado and the mountains. We saw so many things together, including Pikes Peak, Mount Manitou, Seven Falls, and Garden of the Gods. I was a bed-wetter at home for some period, and I remember still having some issues with wetting the bed a little during this trip. I tried to hide it from my grandpa, but I'm sure he noticed; I think we shared a bed in some of our hotels. The good news is it wasn't soaking the bed, just a little pee. Still, yuck. Sorry, Grandpa.

Piano Lessons

I took piano lessons three different times, the first when I was in early grade school, along with Colleen. Our teacher was Mrs. Crose, the pianist at our church. I quit after about a year. I wasn't enjoying it and didn't feel like I was learning to play very well. I hated practicing. A few years later I started up again for a year or two, again with Mrs. Crose. I never really learned to read music, but I became pretty good at memorizing pieces, and could play them relatively well for my teacher during lessons. I'm sure she knew what was going on and wasn't all that surprised that I could play my assigned piece but then couldn't play a new piece she introduced me to during the lesson. I was cheating my way through, not truly learning how to read and play the notes.

I would practice for half an hour a day at my parents' request. I would play for five to seven minutes, decide I wanted a drink, turn off my timer, go get some water and a Fizzie (a flat, pill-shaped flavor-tablet popular at the time) to put in my drink, then watch it fizz as it dissolved. I distinctly remember the root beer flavor. When I went back to the piano I would conveniently knock off a few minutes when I reset the timer, maybe only 20 more minutes, not the 23 to 25 that I really had left. I would get up for something two or three times during each of my practice sessions, probably cutting a full 8 to 10 minutes off my 30-minute practice time. I paid the price in the long run; I never really learned to read music or play the piano well.

In late 1967, when I was 10, I performed at a recital at which each of Mrs. Crose's students played for parents, family, and friends. I had prepared the song "As the Cassons Go Rolling Along." As usual I had

memorized the piece; I had not learned to read the music. When it was my turn I walked up to the front, sat down at the piano, and began to play, very nervously. I feared what people thought of my ability. About midway through the song my mind froze and my capacity shut down when I suddenly hit a wrong note. I couldn't play that song any further even though in my own home or at the teacher's house I could play it easily and perfectly. I immediately stood up from the bench and, with my hands over my face, walked away from the piano to my seat in the auditorium. I was humiliated and embarrassed to be there. I wanted to be somewhere else, somewhere safe and by myself, where people wouldn't judge me. This took place because of one wrong note and a very creative, negative thought in my mind.

Looking back, I'm pretty sure those in the audience hurt with me as I played that one wrong note. They probably hoped I didn't feel too badly about it, and they were looking forward to hearing the rest of the song. Most of them probably felt sorry for me as I left the piano bench, knowing that it must have been hard for me to miss that note. I likely had the empathy and support of those who were there. But that's not how I interpreted it at the time. Instead, the incomplete performance damaged my confidence. I eventually stopped taking lessons.

Later in life I decided that I wanted to take piano lessons again, and at the age of 37 took lessons for another year. This round was not weekly. I had a lot more challenges both in practicing and in making it to lessons when I was working full time and traveling. I remember buying a small keyboard on which to practice my drills. I sometimes practiced with one hand while driving with the other, my little keyboard resting in my lap! I even took that keyboard on work trips. I remember once having a porter help carry my luggage to my room, and as he took a step and swung his arm a little, a sound came from the suitcase. Apparently the instrument had accidentally switched on, and with each step a key was bumped and played. Both of us were surprised by the sound coming from the suitcase.

My First Visit to a Movie Theatre

Bob and I went together to the first movie I remember going to see at a public theater. When I was in fourth grade, at the age of 10, his mom took us to see *The Incredible Mr. Limpet*, starring Don Knotts and an animated fish that he talked with. It was fun to be in a big theater.

Our Radio Station

When I was in fifth grade, Bob and I created a radio station in the driveway for the neighborhood. We owned walkie-talkies that let us talk to someone else on the same frequency. We used these for playing army and many other situations. So for our radio station we put a rubber band around one of our walkie-talkies, covering the transmit key to keep it on permanently. Our friends, at their houses or in their yards, could listen on their walkie-talkies to the same channel to hear the "news" we "broadcasted" from our driveway, and vinyl albums and 45s of the

Monkees and others we played on the large phonograph player we took out to the permanently on walkie-talkie. It was our own full-scale radio station for our local friends to listen to.

Baseball Cards

I became very interested in collecting baseball cards when I was about 10 or 11. I started buying them at the local quick shops (called convenience stores today) that were a little over a mile away: Rexall Drug and another one similar to a Dairy Mart. I would ride my bike to the store, either by myself or with Bob, and buy one, two, or three packs of cards based on how much allowance I had available at the time. We both collected cards for several years. I still have a number of my 1967, '68, '69, '70, and '71 baseball cards. In those days each pack cost five cents for five cards, and they came with a thin bubblegum stick and often one other small decal or printed item. During those years I bought a lot of baseball cards, many basketball cards, some football cards, and a few hockey cards. I still have most of them. A few of them might be worth a good deal now – a lot more than the penny I paid for them.

When we bought new packs we added them to our existing cards, organizing them by teams. We set aside our duplicates – we called them "doubles." We created a game we could play with them that was just like a real baseball game. The cards for one team would be laid out as if each were in its fielding position, and then the other player would put his batters' cards next to the catcher, closest to our hands. We would then shuffle and flip playing cards to learn what each hitter did during their at-bat. An ace was a single, a two a double, a three a triple, and a four a home run. The five, six, and seven cards were strikeouts, and the eight, nine, and ten cards represented groundouts. Jacks, Queens, and Kings were flyouts. We would even flip a coin if we wanted our player to steal a base. A head indicated safety, and a tail indicated being thrown out.

Once one team made three outs, the person with the team in the field would pull all their cards from the table and the other would set up their field for the next inning to begin. We worked hard to select our best possible batting order and fielding positions based on what we knew about each player in real life. We played whole teams against each other; it might be the Astros against the Reds, or any of the other major league baseball teams at the time. We both clearly favored our local St. Louis Cardinals.

We kept track of our teams' win-and-loss records, our home-run leaders, and our stolen-base leaders. One year a guy named Hector Torres on the Houston Astros was our home-run leader. In reality he was a backup player who played nine years in the majors and had only 18 home runs in his whole career, not 50 or 60 or 70 home runs per season like the leaders in the major leagues. It was our version of playing baseball when it was either too cold outside in the winter or too hot in the summer.

I had a large wooden chest – an old jewelry box – that I painted and used to hold my current season's baseball cards. I would carry it to Bob's house and back home when we played in Bob's kitchen with our baseball field spread out across the kitchen table. My special box was located in straightaway center field, and we would each set our fresh 12-ounce Pepsi bottles in the corners of my box. We would get new Pepsis from a wooden crate his family stored in the basement or on the kitchen floor that held 24 bottles of soda. Bob's dad was a gas station owner and he would bring crates of Pepsi home to supply their house. At my house we didn't often drink soda, so playing baseball cards with Bob and drinking our Pepsis was always a special experience for me.

My Tongue Gets Stuck in a Pepsi Bottle

It was easy to create suction between your lips and the opening of a 12-ounce glass Pepsi bottle, and it was fun to feel the pull on your lips as you drank. One day while we were playing, I was drinking from my Pepsi bottle and as the suction increased, my tongue got too close to the mouth of the bottle and was sucked in, forming a U shape as it slid inside. The suction pulled my tongue in as far as it would go, and it was stuck in place inside the bottle. I could see it with my eyes. It was a strong pull, and I couldn't reduce the pressure and release my tongue from the bottle. I was getting scared while Bob sat there laughing! I tried twisting and turning the bottle, and then my tongue, but it was totally stuck. I tried to ask Bob for help, despite his laughing, but he couldn't understand me because I couldn't use my tongue to articulate my words. After what seemed like a half hour but was probably only 20 seconds, I created an air path through the U-shape of my tongue and slid my tongue out of the bottle. It was a scary, crazy experience I can laugh about now, but at the time it had me really concerned, fearing I was going to be stuck that way forever. I wondered if we would have to shatter the glass bottle to break the suction.

This experience sure caught me by surprise. Suddenly my attention was not on our game. I don't know who won that round, but I know that I won by having my tongue back when it was finally freed from that powerful glass soda bottle.

I continued to drink a lot of sodas from those bottles back in the 1970s, and now occasionally in the 2020s. Most bottles have been replaced by cans and plastic bottles of various sizes, and maybe for good reason, as this might have also happened to others. But I've never heard of anyone else who's had this experience.

Street Hockey

There was a phase when my friends and I played a lot of street hockey just up the street. The brand-new professional hockey team, the St. Louis Blues, was founded in 1967, when I was 10 and just starting fifth grade. Everyone was so excited about the new franchise. Ray and Tom's dad created hockey nets using wire and metal frames that we set up right in the middle of the street. We set one up at Ray and Tom's driveway and another two houses down the street. We all wore roller skates clamped onto our shoes, and we all had hockey sticks, some of us even hockey gloves. We would either skate or run as we played three-on-three or four-on-four hockey right in the middle of our street, moving our metal nets whenever a car headed toward us. We had a blast playing together for hours out there. We just had to watch out for big Billy Shounhoffer with his amazing, sizzling slap shot that would send our hollow plastic orange puck slicing through the air toward the goal, or at least in that general direction. When it hit one of us it really stung, but it was worth it for all the enjoyment we got from playing.

Gone for Hours

During the summers throughout grade school I would be gone for hours playing with my friends. There were no cell phones to keep parents and children in touch. I just needed to be home for lunch and dinner. We played baseball, basketball, wiffle ball, football, and hockey in the street nearby, at one of the fields at St. Jude Catholic School a half mile away, at the Veterans of Foreign Wars field, or in a friend's backyard. We played for hours without contact with our parents; we felt safe and they felt we were safe as well, within the tribe of our friends.

During the school year my friends and I would be gone for hours after school, during the afternoons and into the evenings. We were out and about most of the time, playing with our friends.

Weeping Willow Tree

Just down the street and around the corner was a large weeping willow tree that we climbed and played in for hours. It was in Kenny Olsen's backyard. Kenny was several years younger than I, but was a fun, crazy young kid who loved to hang around and play sports with us. We played hours of wiffle ball in his backyard, with the home plate just beyond the base of that weeping willow tree.

Playing 21

We played a lot of basketball in my backyard. It created a large dirt spot in the yard, about 15 by 20 feet, with a lot of pounded dirt. At times I would shoot alone. We played HORSE, PIG, and one-on-one basketball games – sometimes even two-on-two – but there wasn't enough room for bigger teams.

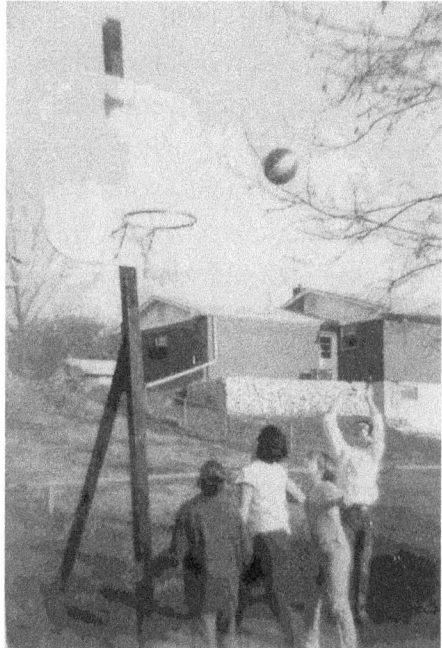

We also played a lot of 21. For 21, you shoot to score 21 points, and you have to hit exactly 21. You're guarded by the others playing with you; it could be one person or several. You start at about where the three-point line would be, dribbling and trying to get off a shot while others guard you. If you make a basket you earn two points and are awarded three shots from the free-throw line without anyone guarding you; the others line up under the basket to try to get the rebound if you miss. If you hit a free throw you earn one more point. So if you hit all three of your free throws you earn three points, and you get to take the ball back out near the three-point line and start working for another two-point shot. If you miss the shot the other players go for the rebound and shoot their shot from wherever they gathered the rebound, be it close or far away because of a big bounce off the basket. If they hit that shot they earn two points and are entitled to shoot up to three free throws for more points. If by chance the person with the highest score earns a point that puts them over 21, they're sent back to 13 points. This process continues until someone reaches 21 and wins.

We created a league out of this backyard game. We kept track of how many points each of us scored and how many wins we had. It got quite obsessive. We would even intentionally go over 21 to score more points. If you went over 21 you went back to 13, and then scored even more points as you tried to get back up to 21. So if you get to 21 you actually score a total of 30 points for that one game. We were into the details and tracked all of our statistics.

I played 21 with many kids in the neighborhood, but none more than with little Kenny Olsen. He would come over to our house and knock on the door to see if I was available to come out and play 21 with him, and we'd play for hours on end. Over the years that we played 21 in our backyard, probably 70 percent of the time it was just the two of us playing. We loved our 21.

Kevin

Kevin was a friend I met in grade school. We loved to play basketball together at school. We were a great two-man team. He moved to another school district a couple of years later, and I didn't see him again until we were both in our junior year of high school, about five years later. He had been taller than I and had grown even much taller by the time he was a junior. I enjoyed learning that he was his high school's team captain and leading scorer. He stayed with basketball, and it sure paid off for him.

The Boy Scouts

I joined the Cub Scouts, Webelos, and Boy Scouts. I went through the motions and earned my 2nd Class badge in the Boy Scouts, but even that was due primarily to an incentive my parents offered me: They would buy me a new baseball glove if I achieved that level. I could have learned so much more from these scouting programs, but my heart was not in it. I enjoyed the overnight campouts, but the weekly meetings didn't do much for me, except that we met in the gym at Mount Pleasant Elementary School. I would ride my bike and show up half an hour early to play basketball in the gym and stay at least half an hour after the meeting so I could play more basketball.

Basketball Down the Street

In addition to all the basketball that I played in my backyard, I also discovered that a house about six houses down from us had a basketball hoop on its long two-lane driveway. My friends and I played on that driveway with the younger boy who lived there, Jeffrey. His parents allowed us to play there even when Jeffery wasn't available. I played a lot of basketball at their house. The driveway was big enough for us to play two-on-two or three-on-three on a concrete surface instead of on the dirt in my backyard. I was so thankful that they allowed us the freedom to use their nice concrete driveway. In a sense they were paying it forward, because in turn Carolyn and I let our next-door neighbor's kids play hours of basketball on the court in our backyard. We're providing the same service to them that I received when I was growing up.

A Walk to Bill Bridges' House

While I was in the Boy Scouts a friend and I walked five miles down Page Avenue and back home to earn a merit badge. I had two motives in this case. We walked along a long major road out to Maryland Heights to the home of my favorite St. Louis Hawks basketball player. We were lucky; Bill Bridges was home and signed his autograph on the corner of an envelope for me. It was a win-win investment: I earned my merit badge in Scouts and personally met and received the autograph of my favorite player.

Coaching Girls' Softball

One summer I joined my friend Bob in helping his mom, Dot, coach a girls' softball team. That was a lot of fun. I must have been about 12 at the time, in sixth grade.

Sports Schedules

After I fell in love with baseball and basketball, I started to collect season schedules from various professional sports teams. I would write a letter to the Chamber of Commerce of a city and ask them to mail me a copy of their season schedule. For example, I wrote to the Atlanta Chamber of Commerce and requested a copy of the Atlanta Hawks' schedule for that season. They would then mail me a small, multicolored, multifolded pocket team schedule, small enough to put in a wallet. I collected these schedules from many teams. It was so fun to get a new schedule in the mail. I don't think I held on to any of them. It was a fun activity for a guy who loved sports. These days a Chamber of Commerce would probably not even respond, assuming I can look up the schedule on the internet.

Color TV

We had a black-and-white TV for years while I was in grade school. I remember the exciting news that Bob's family had purchased a color TV – it was the first time I had the chance to watch a show in color. It was amazing. I could hardly believe it was real. I watched several shows at Bob's over the next couple of years before we also purchased a color TV for our house.

Stuck in the Sewer

One day while we were broadcasting our radio station to the neighborhood, two of our friends, who were being babysat by a neighbor three houses down from theirs, decided they wanted to listen to our show. They came out of the house, walked across the yard and down to the street, and sat on the sewer platform so they could see us better and hear our show. They were having trouble getting our station to come in, so they removed the back of the walkie-talkie to check the battery. Unfortunately the walkie-talkie's back fell into the sewer. To see where it was, the younger of them lay down on the street and slid his head between the sewer platform and the street to see if he could see the back of the walkie-talkie. He couldn't get his head far enough in to see it, so he started to pull his head out, only to learn that he was stuck with his head in the crack of the sewer. He tried and tried but couldn't get his head out. He cried for help. We saw what was happening, so we quickly grabbed our walkie-talkie and ran over to provide a newscast of the event.

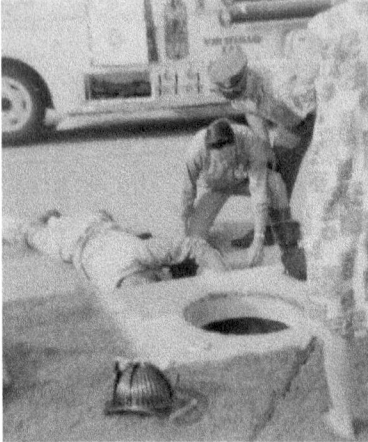

The babysitter was very frustrated about what the kids had done. They weren't supposed to have gone out to the street. Because we couldn't help him get his head out of the sewer crack, she eventually called the fire department, which arrived a few minutes later with a large fire truck. This had become a significant event. They tried to maneuver his head to help get it out of the sewer, but that didn't work. They tried putting vaseline on the sides of his head, and that didn't work. They eventually used a jack to raise the sewer platform a little off the street, and he was able to slide his head out. It had to be terrifying to be stuck with your head between two slabs of concrete and not be able to get it out. We broadcast the whole event from our walkie-talkie, but probably no

one else heard any of it. It's likely our only two listeners were battling the head-stuck-in-the-sewer dilemma. It was quite a memorable event for all of us.

Music

During the last few years of grade school I listened to popular music on my transistor radio, tuning in to local stations like KSLQ. It wasn't until my later years of high school and my college years that I spent a lot of time enjoying music – groups like The Eagles, America, Bread, and the Carpenters.

As a high school senior and into college I started listening to more contemporary Christian music than I had in the past. I enjoyed musicians such as The 2nd Chapter of Acts, Honeytree, Lovesong, Lamb, Paul Clark, Phil Keaggy, Keith Green, Randy Stonehill, and Larry Norman. I spent a lot of time enjoying the sounds and meditating on the words of many of their songs. They reinforced my spiritual beliefs, which I had been taught in church and read about in my Bible, but with a modern, generally soft-rock sound. I listened to music on my transistor radio and on vinyl records and record albums, or LPs – for Long Play, that spun at different speeds on a turntable: 33 1/3rd, 45, and 78 revolutions per minute (rpm), or how many times the record spun in a minute. I also used an 8-track player; an "8-track" was a recording on a roll of magnetic tape wrapped around two spools inside a plastic casing. These units were "continuous

play"; once the tape finished it would start over. Later, cassettes were developed. They were also magnetic tape wound in a plastic case, but they were smaller and simpler in design. Finally CDs were developed. These were all before today's digital recordings on SD cards and jump drives, and streaming music and video to our devices.

Climbing Trees

Climbing trees and swinging on vines were other ways my friends and I spent our days. We would pretend we were Tarzan or an army platoon hiding out from the enemy. There were vines that we could either cross or swing from. It was so fun to be 15 or 20 feet above the ground, crossing from one tree to the next in one of the two densely wooded areas that were just up the street from my house. They were sandwiched between two housing developments and an undeveloped area whose owner we didn't know. The wooded areas were maybe only 40 feet wide and 100 feet deep. They were our forests, our playgrounds, and no one ever chased us out of them.

The Storm Sewers

This is the story that sparked the idea for this book. We had a storm sewer opening right in front of our house. Since we were constantly playing with balls in our yard and on the street, it was

common for one to roll down the sewer opening at the edge of our street. That meant we often lifted and set aside the large, heavy, round, rusted iron sewer lid so one of us could climb down into the storm sewer to retrieve the ball we had lost. Sometimes it would be me climbing down into that sewer.

Over time, and having become familiar with going down into the sewer pipe, we began to explore where the large horizontal concrete pipe went. We learned that it connected to the sewer opening down the street and around the bend, and then we learned about its connection to another sewer opening. We eventually started exploring farther and farther, walking through these large sewer pipes. I'm guessing they were about five feet in diameter.

Sometimes we had to walk up on the sides of the pipes to avoid the water that pooled in the bottom three or four inches. We would run through the pipes, chase each other, hide, and explore, till one day we reached the end of the pipe, down several streets, where the storm water flowed out into a little creek. After that we sometimes went down to the creek and entered that way instead. We spent hours exploring this underground playground.

We were never in those pipes during a flood or when water was rushing. We felt safe and like this was simply a large, cylindrical, concrete playground. It probably wasn't all that clean, but we never touched the bottom, just the sides, unless we were retrieving a ball that was sitting in a puddle at the bottom of the pipe. I think my parents knew we played there, but I'm not sure.

Bicycles

We rode our bikes a lot, and all over our neighborhood. I would ride a mile or more away, to my grade school, to friends' houses, to the VFW field to play baseball, to the drug stores to buy baseball cards, and to explore the streets around me. I enjoyed riding "free hands" down our street. I once ran into another bike and flipped over, scratching myself up pretty badly. I wasn't paying attention.

Sometimes I clipped doubles of my baseball cards to my bike frame with a clothespin, sticking into the wheel spokes just enough so the end of the card would flap on each spoke when the wheel turned, making a repeated thap, thap, thap sound, kind of like the sound of a motor.

Wiffle Ball

We played a lot of wiffle ball in the street in front of our house. Wiffle ball is basically like playing baseball, just with a hollow, plastic bat and a hard plastic ball with air holes around the side. It would act like a baseball, but wouldn't go as far or cause as much damage if it hit someone or something. It would usually just bounce off whatever it hit. It gave us the ability to play ball without seriously damaging things. At times we received some complaints from neighbors because we hit a house or a car, but it didn't usually dent or break anything. We would average between six and ten of us playing together. We needed at least three on each team.

Our street had a sharp left turn two houses down, and it widened there as well, creating a large, open concrete area where we played. Straight ahead toward the curve was the Crawfords' front yard and house, with a large picture window facing the street. We would set home plate right in front of my house, near the sewer, and then first, second, and third base would be set up in that open part of the street, with the outfield being the distant part of the curve of the street and, of course, the Crawfords' front yard. The Crawfords had two kids, Kitra and Shawn. Shawn was a little younger than I, but since he sometimes played with us that made it more acceptable for us to hit balls into his yard at times. We spent hours playing wiffle ball there in the street, stepping aside each time a car came driving through. We were thankful that no one parked vehicles on the street in the area where we played.

We also played wiffle ball in the backyard of Marty and Terry's house. They had a nice large backyard, just two houses down from us. And we played at Kenny Olson's house, with home plate next to the big weeping willow tree we loved to climb. Our field was essentially his backyard and the yard next to his. The far end of Kenny's yard and that next-door neighbor's yard had a pretty steep incline, so not many balls went very far into that neighbor's yard. Both Kenny's yard and Marty and Terry's yard were pretty torn up with all of us kids playing hours of wiffle ball.

Flies-and-Grounders

We played flies-and-grounders in Bob's backyard and over his fence to the next yard. Someone would pitch a wiffle ball, a softball, or a baseball. Another person was the batter. Another player or two would be in another portion of Bob's yard or in the neighbor's yard beyond the fence. We would score a run anytime a batter hit the ball, moving an imaginary runner to first, second, and third base, and finally home. Our imaginary runners would advance a base when those in the field couldn't field the ball on the ground or catch it in the air. If they did get it, it was considered an out. After the batter reached three outs, each position would rotate from outfield to infield to pitcher, and finally to being the batter. We played this game for hours.

I do have one vivid memory of our friend Ray hitting a pitch right into the large basement picture window facing outwards

towards Bob's backyard, smashing it. It just so happened that Ray's dad was watching from Ray's backyard, and he called out, "That's my boy!" in frustration. I'm sure it cost a lot of money to replace that large window. I think we were outlawed from playing flies-and-grounders in Bob's yard from that point on, at least with a baseball or softball.

Hot Box

Hot box was another fun game that we played with a ball and glove, often a baseball. It required at least three people, but not more than five. We would select two locations as our bases: our tree in the front yard and either our mailbox or the low brick frame of a lamppost that was near the end of our sidewalk where it approached the driveway. Sometimes all three locations would serve as bases. One player with a glove would stand at each of the bases, and they would play catch. A third person would run the bases, trying, as in baseball, to steal a base and advance to the next base without being tagged with the ball. If a player made an overthrow, it would be easy for the runner to run from base to base many times to get credit for achieving many stolen bases. If the throws were all good, the runner or runners would take a lead from their base when the ball was in the hands of the person at the other base. The runner would try to lure the other person to throw the ball to the runner's base, and then take off as fast as they could to the base the ball had been thrown from. It was so fun to play, and the runner was seldom hit in the back with the ball – maybe sometimes. Sometimes we played with two bases and one runner, and sometimes with three bases and one or two runners. We played this game many times in various places in the neighborhood. We enjoyed our versions of playing baseball in areas smaller than a whole baseball field.

Baseball

CHRIS WARNKY

GIANTS

Chris Warnky

OUTFIELD—1ST

We played hours of baseball for months on end at St. Jude Catholic Church, either on one of their baseball diamonds or sometimes on the rough soccer field. It was only about a half mile away, just up the street and down the walking path to the school and church. We also played at the VFW post, which was almost a mile away. We usually rode our bikes to that field, which meant crossing one busy road. There we played with many other kids from several different neighborhoods.

In seventh grade I played organized baseball on a formal team at St. Jude. I played one season, getting a white-and-green uniform, a team picture, a few at-bats, and some plays in the outfield. I didn't play very well, and I also had a hard time following the fast pitches that were coming at me.

My Bird

I was off playing wiffle ball in Kenny Olsen's backyard with a number of my friends. It was a great game. We were having so much fun, when all of a sudden I heard Colleen yelling from across the yard, "You need to feed your bird!" I yelled back, "What?" because I was really focused on our game. She said, "You have to come home now to feed your bird." I asked, "Really, now?" "Yes," was the reply. I apologized to my friends because I would have to leave and cross the two yards and the street to my house to feed my stupid bird, a little yellow-and-green parakeet. I quickly ran home, opened the door, ran through the living room and into the kitchen, and immediately pulled out the food cup from the side of the cage, dumped it, wiped it out, and then poured new seed in the container, trying not to spill, which would cost me even more time if I had to clean it up. Then I slid it back into the cage. I was one-third of the way done. I reached over to the other side of the cage and filled the water cup so my bird could drink when it needed to – two down, one to go. I needed to clean the base of the cage by pulling out the tray at the bottom, dumping it, wiping it down, and then putting a new paper towel down so if the bird pooped it wouldn't land on the tray and require even more cleanup. All I could think of was that I was missing my wiffle ball game. I wanted so badly to get back there quickly. As I started to pull out the tray, I noticed something lying at the bottom. It was my bird; it had

died and was lying there on the bottom of the cage. My mind quickly went to the question of how much longer it was going to take me to get rid of the bird. I don't remember the rest of this story, but I probably wrapped the bird in a paper towel and threw it in the outside trash, and I probably eventually made it back to the whiffle ball game, if it was still going on, but upon reflection I acknowledged that my love for sports was truly way more love than I had for a pet. I think the bird was my parents' attempt to help me learn to take some responsibility. I'm not sure I ever really wanted a bird, at least not very much. I might have voiced an interest once while we were at a pet store, but that was surely as far as it went. This episode confirmed clearly for me that I really wasn't a pet-loving guy. Some kids are, but I sure wasn't. For me it was back to my game of wiffle ball.

Shooting Firecrackers and M-80s

My friends and I used to buy and light some very exciting fireworks in our neighborhood with our friends. An M-80 was a very powerful, large firecracker. I specifically remember one of my friends setting off an M-80 and throwing it toward me! It didn't hit me or burn me, but boy was it loud!

School at Fee Fee Baptist Church

During part of my sixth grade I was bused several miles away to Fee Fee Baptist Church to attend school (Fee Fee is a historic name from the neighborhood). Our Mount Pleasant school building was being remodeled. The administration negotiated with that church to rent and use some of their classrooms for part of the year.

Playing Pool with My Aunt Jean

I think it was primarily on Saturday mornings, but I remember playing pool in our basement with my Aunt Jean on our old, cheap pool table. It was okay, but not great. It didn't have a hard slate or marble tabletop; it was made of plywood. But we had fun playing eight-ball and stripes-and-solids, two pretty simple yet fun games of pool.

Hanley Hills Baptist Church

We attended Hanley Hills Baptist Church for at least 10 years of my childhood, up through high school. It was five miles from our house. The other kids who attended with their parents lived in different school districts, Normandy and Ritenour. There was only one other family with kids who attended my school. Other than at church, I didn't play or interact with any of the other kids there, and none of them became close friends.

Church Choir

When I was 13, in seventh grade, I was in the youth choir at Hanley Hills Baptist Church, and I had my first speaking assignment. I had a speaking part at the end of one of the songs, saying, "Sorry about that!" It was pretty simple, but it was a new experience to be in front of a crowd, and a big deal for me to say it at just the right time.

That choir also took a few bus trips to sing at other churches. We performed the musical *Tell It Like It Is*. On one trip those in the back of the bus decided it would be fun to see how many of us we could get into the little bathroom in the back corner of the bus. We kept pushing more people in. I was one of the top ones because I was one of the smaller people in the group. All of a sudden I heard, "Get out! Get out!" We apparently put too many people in that bathroom and too much pressure on the back corner window. It had popped out onto the street, and we didn't want anyone to fall out. The leaders at the front didn't know it had happened, but they were going to find out eventually, so someone shared the news. I think our group was required to generate the money to pay for the window, and I'm sure some of the older people on the trip probably got quite a reprimand.

Around-the-Table Ping Pong

We enjoyed playing around-the-table ping pong, played with several people lined up around a ping-pong table. One person hits the ball and then sets the paddle down on the table, running to the end of the line on the other side of the table. Then the person behind them in line picks up the paddle and hits the ball, then sets the paddle down for the next person to pick up. The pattern is repeated until someone misses the ball. It can be exhausting and fun. When you miss the ball, you get a letter of a word. Once you have enough letters to spell the entire word that was selected, such as P.I.N.G., you're out and must sit down, reducing the number of players. When you're down to the last two players, the game changes. You hit the ball, set the paddle down, turn around, and then pick up the paddle to hit the ball again. You repeat this process until someone has completely spelled the whole word. The person who is left is the winner. We played a lot of around-the-table ping pong in the basement of our home, and we introduced the game to many others in various other places.

A Gun at the Front Door

This is not technically my story, but I'll share it anyway. One night we heard our doorbell ring. Colleen and I were sitting on the couch in our living room. Colleen got up to answer the door, and to her surprise and shock, a person wearing a mask had a gun pointed right at her, demanding, "Stick 'em up!" It sent Colleen into a loud cry and fit. It was so scary that her jaw locked open and she couldn't relieve the pressure to close her mouth. It was a traumatic experience for her in particular, and for us as a family.

As the drama unfolded, we discovered that a neighborhood girl was trying to play a practical joke on us. She used a Halloween mask and a play silver cowboy gun, but to Colleen it sure looked real in the moment. It was no joke to us; it was such a scary experience for our entire family, and especially for Colleen. We were so mad at her for doing that. This experience sure made the point that you should never play a practical joke on anyone using anything that looks like a weapon.

Crushes

The first time I remember caring about or being interested in girls was at Hanley Hills Baptist Church. I was probably around seven or eight at the time. I was interested in the little blond daughter of our church music director, Lynn. I once took a photo of her, and that was all I was willing to do with her. A few years later I noticed Diane, another girl at the church. She attended my school district but became involved with a bad crowd that had poor habits, which led to them and her often getting into trouble, especially at school. I was way too shy to take any initiative with either of these girls. I liked them, or was interested, but that was it.

My Unicycle

I learned to ride a unicycle my parents had bought for me when I was in the fourth or fifth grade, probably around the age of 10 or 11. I'm not sure why I became so interested in learning to ride it but I learned to stay on it by leaning on our ping-pong table in the basement as I slowly pedaled my way around it. The seat of the unicycle was banged up in the front and the back – that black-and-white seat had fallen to the ground so many times from my falls. I was eventually able to move to the street, holding on to our mailbox to get onto the unicycle. Then I would practice, slowly improving – one complete turn of the pedals, then eventually two, then three or more. Then I could ride the distance of our whole yard or more. I learned to ride it fairly well. I could ride it while dribbling or shooting a basketball, and catching a ball, and a few other tricks, but not much more than that.

When I got older I rode my unicycle throughout the neighborhood, and when I was a junior and senior in high school, sometimes even to my job at McDonald's a few miles away. I also rode it to some of my college classes and to our early morning prayer meetings at the church.

My dad also learned to ride the unicycle. I still have it today. I haven't ridden it very often, but I can still ride it.

Chapter 5

Junior High Years, Grades Seven and Eight

These activities were from the summer of 1968, after I had graduated from sixth grade, through the spring of 1970 when I graduated from eighth grade. This is when I was 12 through the first part of my 14th year.

Report Card Trouble

Back to the topic of school and grades, there was one semester in junior high when I earned four Ds on my report card. I use the term *earned* because I truly deserved each of the Ds. If I remember correctly, the classes were English, math, social studies, and science. It was a terrible performance on my part. It clearly reflected that I had no interest whatsoever in school and learning. I put no effort into it. I was just there to get by and get through so that I could get back home and have fun playing the sports I loved.

That report card opened my parents' eyes, and they took a strong new stance with me about my schooling, grounding me for several months. I wasn't allowed to go out and play until I finished all my homework and completed my chores. During that time I couldn't listen to or watch any sports! I was also required to read for 30 minutes each day. I remember reading books like *Trouble After School*, *Tunnel through Time*, and some sports-related stories by Matt Christopher. I also started reading many of the books in the

Encyclopedia Brown child-detective series. My parents were taking a strong stance to try to turn around my poor academic performance.

I already hated reading, and this new requirement made it even more frustrating and depressing. I hated reading tremendously, partly because I read so slowly and poorly, and partly because it had become my latest and most frustrating penalty. I felt like I had died when all my sports were cut off, because that had been my life.

But all of these new requirements worked to some degree, and by the next semester I had significantly improved my grades. These penalties helped me face the harsh reality of how poor my attitude toward school was at that time and how much my life was wrapped up in the enjoyment of playing, watching, and listening to sports.

I hope my young readers don't let other things squeeze out your opportunities to learn and grow, developing yourself so that it benefits you for the rest of your life.

Crushes

I had mild crushes on some girls during this time, such as Patty, a very conservatively dressed girl who was in a couple of my classes. I don't believe that I ever even talked to her. And, also, Gail and Lynn Finley at our church. I was first interested in Gail, then in her younger sister, Lynn. I thought about them and would ride my bike about three miles to where they lived in another school district, and ride near or by their home hoping to see them, but I didn't want to be noticed. I never took any action to convey my interest in them, but I liked them.

Pattonville Basketball Camp

As you now know, I loved basketball and played a lot of it in our neighborhood. I talked to my parents about paying for me to participate in the high school basketball camp to improve my skills. I enjoyed the camp, which was tough, and it allowed me to meet several upperclassmen on the high school basketball team. They were my heroes; I looked up to them. And I learned a lot at the camp, which increased my confidence.

Junior High Basketball

In seventh grade, when I was 12, I tried out for the junior high basketball team. Well over 50 kids were trying out for the 12 spots on the team. I participated in the first couple of tryouts, but then came down with a bad cold that kept me out for most of the remaining practices. By the time the coaches decided who they would cut, I had survived to the final 15, but was one of the final three players cut from the team. This was very discouraging. I believe that if I hadn't come down with a cold I might very well have been one of those selected to be on the team. Several of my friends who made the team felt sorry for me and believed I should have made it. That, at least, was encouraging.

I continued to try out for the school basketball team in eighth, ninth, and tenth grades, but after that I gave up, believing I had fallen too far behind my friends who had continued to develop under high school coaching. Starting when I was in ninth grade, over 100 people tried out for the team as the two junior high teams merged into one Pattonville High School team. Our high school had well over 2,500 students, and we had 880 in just my class.

I loved and still love basketball, but playing on the school team didn't work out.

Managing Basketball

After being cut from the basketball tryouts each year, I volunteered to be a manager so I could spend time with the guys who got to play the game I loved. I attended each practice, assisted the coaches with the players, and shot baskets on my own. It was fun to attend and support all the games, both home and away. I helped with warm-ups, made shot charts, and kept statistics.

Chapter 6

High School Years, Grades Nine through Twelve

These activities spanned the summers of 1971 through 1975, my high school years. This is when I was 14 through the first part of my 18th year.

Slick

My parents purchased a puppy that we named Slick. I don't even know the type of dog he was. I think Colleen and Mark spent much more time with him. I was in my mid-to-late high school years and I didn't have any time for him or interest in him. I knew he was around, but that was about it.

I went off to college not thinking or caring about Slick. One weekend when I was back in town visiting my family I decided to shoot some baskets in our backyard. As I dribbled and shot, Slick kept getting in the way, probably wanting my attention. At one point I used my foot to move him out of the way so I could dribble. I didn't kick him, but lifted him away from the court with my foot. In frustration I yelled out at him, "Stay out of the way, Slick, I'm trying to play some basketball." He was now an older dog and was larger than when we first bought him. One of my siblings was within earshot and called out to me, "That's not Slick, it's Matt. Slick died. Matt's our second dog." My lack of attention and interest in animals was again revealed. I didn't even realize he was a different dog. I think they were similar in look and size, but this *was* a different dog, and I hadn't noticed. I have never been interested in dogs or animals as pets.

Church Basketball Team

When I was a sophomore, at the age of 15 in 1972, I played one year on our Hanley Hills Baptist Church boys' basketball team. We had red jerseys. I started at the guard position. I recall that one of the older boys on the team, Eugene, was drafted into the military a couple of years later during the Vietnam War. He was killed in action. That was a sad message to hear.

During one of our games I dove for a loose basketball on the floor, showing my dedication, and two other players lunged for it as well. I don't remember who took possession, but I was hurt getting sandwiched between the two. My shoulder hurt, and I don't think I played the rest of

the game. It continued to sting that night and into the next morning. My parents decided to have a doctor look at it. They took X-rays and discovered I had fractured my left collarbone. That was the first and only time that I know of that I've broken a bone. They put me in a shoulder brace to relieve the stress on the joint and allow the bone to heal. I had to lie low for over a week. I wore that brace for about six weeks, but it didn't stop my athletic activities. I remember playing volleyball during gym classes using one arm and one hand. I also played a good deal of basketball with just my right arm and hand. I was able to develop the skill of controlling the ball pretty well with just one hand. But I no longer dove to the floor after a ball during this healing period.

Putt-a-Way Miniature Golf Course Job

My first out-of-the-house job was working for my Uncle Rick. He had recently purchased an old, run-down miniature golf course and was refurbishing it. He was replacing all the carpet and painting all the features at each hole. He hired several kids at low hourly pay to help complete this process. I was one of the kids he hired.

I was the youngest of them; most were out of high school. It was 1972, the summer after I finished ninth grade, when I was 15. I was paid a dollar an hour and worked nearly 10 hours a day for a week. I helped remove the old carpet and glue, and then measured, cut, and installed the new carpet at each hole. I also assisted in painting the various features at each hole. There were about six of us. It was hard work, but I had my first job and I was making money. At the end of that week I had made almost $60.00! I now knew what it was like to work and be paid for it. This was much different from getting paid a quarter or two for doing chores around the house.

Denny's Job

My first job with a large company was as a busboy at our local Denny's restaurant, about two miles from our house. I would soon be turning 16 and was in 10th grade. When I started I didn't have my driver's license, so my parents took me to work. I started with evening shifts a couple of days a week, working 6:00 to 9:00 PM, cleaning tables. After I received my driver's license, I started working weekends – the graveyard shift. What's a graveyard shift? That's the shift that runs from 11:00 PM to 7:00 AM. It was a long shift that required a significant adjustment to my schedule.

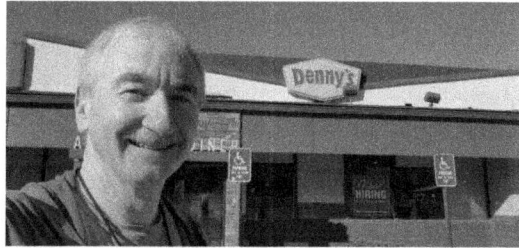

For months I worked graveyard shifts on Friday and Saturday nights. It was grueling. The late-night wild crowd came in from midnight till maybe 3:00 or later in the morning. After that time the customers trailed off. Working that shift had a tremendously negative impact on my ability to stay awake during the day through at least Monday or Tuesday. Each week I had to try to reset my sleep schedule to be during the night.

This job was a lot of physical labor, standing on my feet for hours and carrying dirty dishes throughout my shift, for not much money. I made $1.60 an hour, below the minimum wage because I also received tips from the waitresses, which could be another $2.00 to $3.00 per shift. At home I would jokingly pick up our corded telephone from its wall stand and pretend to dial, saying, "Mr. Denny, I quit." To this day, my dad still remembers this and jokes about it.

Being my first formal job, I also learned a lot from it. I worked for two or three weeks before I realized that employees were given breaks. I had worked straight through my shifts whether they were three or eight hours long. As I paid attention to others, I eventually noticed they were taking breaks during their shifts and even getting a 15- to 20-minute lunch break, taking advantage of the food benefit that was also provided, typically a nice whole serving of one of the entrees listed on the menu. Somehow, during orientation – or the lack of it – I missed the fact that we were provided breaks. A few weeks in I began to take advantage of those as well, which helped stave off fatigue.

Working at Denny's was an eye-opener on so many fronts, and it negatively impacted my performance at school. Still, it allowed me to earn enough money to pay for my car and insurance, which were the two necessities my parents required of me if I was going to drive.

Sleeping during Classes

So I slept through many of my classes during my junior year of high school. I was worn out from my overnight shifts at Denny's. I developed a terrible habit that followed me through the rest of my high school experience. I attended each class, paying attention at the start of the lecture, but often fell asleep with my arms crossed on my desktop. I woke as I heard the bell go off, signaling the end of the period. I frequently found a puddle of drool on my desk that I would wipe up with the sleeve of my shirt. I would quickly glance at the chalkboard to see if our assignment was listed, and if so I wrote it down. Active classes kept me awake, such as art, shop, some science classes with labs, and of course gym. But I had a tough time staying awake during lectures. These behaviors caused another significant setback in my school performance. Working at Denny's took a considerable toll on my education.

The Living Bible

I started reading a green, soft-covered, paraphrased version of the Bible in about 1972, when I was a sophomore in high school. It was called *The Living Bible*. It was first published in 1971. It used modern English in contrast to the more challenging King James Version, which used the formal English from its 1611 original. I felt like I could really understand *The Living Bible*. I knew it wasn't a literal translation of the original manuscripts but was written to consistently convey their intent in a way that someone from the 1970s could easily understand. The *thees* and *thous* were replaced with more up-to-date wording.

This was the first time I truly devoted myself to reading the Bible on my own. I had read it for years as part of traditional church services, but now I really understood and related well to it on my own.

Fast-forward to the 2020s, and I currently read the *New Living Translation*, which is an actual translation but much easier to read. It was first published in 1996.

I Loved Sports

Have I convinced you that I loved sports? I even took an English class named Cars and Sports. It allowed me to learn the basics of English with a sports slant, so the books I read were about sports and cars, and each writing assignment was centered on one or the other. To this day Carolyn gives me grief about how much easier that English class must have been than the others that were offered. It catered to people like me who really didn't have much interest in school.

McDonald's Job

Within a year I had quit Denny's and was hired by McDonald's, the fast-food hamburger restaurant. I worked there for over two years, flipping hamburgers and working the front counter. I became an expert at cooking hamburgers.

I worked there during McDonald's 20th anniversary, back in 1975, just before I graduated from high school. On that day McDonald's offered 10-cent hamburgers. I worked more than 10 hours that day, all at the grill cooking hamburgers. I cooked just over 10,000 hamburgers on that one day. I kept track of the 300 hamburger-patty boxes I worked through. I would lay out 12 hamburgers on the grill at a time – six in each hand – and repeat this process four times, resulting in 48 burgers at various stages of cooking. I would lay 12 burgers on the grill; sear 12 that were already there, pressing a burger turner across the top of each; flip the next 12 that were cooking, then salt them; and finally pull the 12 that were done, placing them on buns. Then I would clean that section of the grill with a scraper, lay out another set of 12, and start the process all over again. It was quite a mass-production process.

I worked with many coworkers from the Ritenour school district. Given the location of the McDonald's, I only had a few coworkers from my school, Pattonville. I was offered a promotion to a management position at that restaurant, but I informed them that I planned to go to college and wouldn't be accepting the offer.

St. Louis University Basketball Camp

I believe it was between my sophomore and junior year that my parents paid for and took me to the St. Louis University week-long summer basketball camp. I enjoyed these daytime sessions, continuing to learn and grow in my basketball skills, which I loved playing even if I wasn't on the high school team. Some of the St. Louis University basketball team starters helped work the camp. They were impressive to me.

Drawing Portraits

I enjoyed drawing even in early grade school. I would draw various cartoon characters from the comics and also have fun drawing active sports figures running, jumping, and playing football, baseball, and basketball. As I entered high school my love of sports led me to draw large portraits of my favorite athletes, particularly basketball and baseball players. I have also drawn many family members and celebrities, as well as whatever caught my fancy.

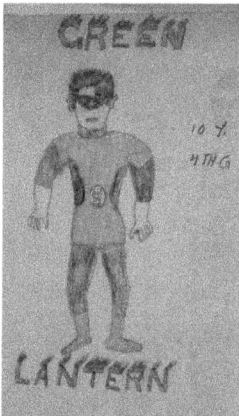

In high school I took a drawing class with Mrs. Jones, and she helped me develop my drawing skills, especially with charcoal and chalk. I increased the amount of drawing I did during this period. I spent many hours in my basement bedroom with a 24-by-18-inch piece of sheetrock as my drawing surface, with masking tape applied around the edges to keep the dust from spreading. I would prop it on my lap, lean it forward onto my desk,

take out a large sheet of portrait paper, and start drawing a portrait of another one of my favorite sports figures, hour upon hour while I listened to either music or one of my favorite sporting events, either a basketball or baseball game.

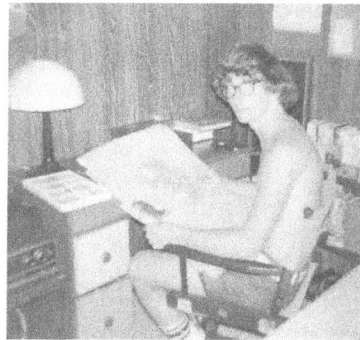

I was one of the top two or three students in our drawing class. I would complete my portraits very well and quickly, almost one per class. The other top student was a perfectionist, with meticulous attention to detail in his work. I would complete five portraits in the time it took him to complete one, but his were much better than mine. I didn't have the patience to be a perfectionist, but my portraits still turned out quite well. I had the opportunity to frame some of them, and they were hung in the hallway of the high school's art wing. That was a great opportunity to showcase my talent. I also had the chance in college to display over 20 of my sports portraits at the Union Center at Southeast Missouri State University.

Drawing has been an enjoyable part of my life. As an adult I hadn't drawn for many years, but at one point Carolyn asked me to draw portraits of each of our kids to display in our home. I did, and each of them has hung in our family room for years now. I took photos of all my portraits, and I have a photo album dedicated to them. I still have all of my original portraits stored away in my bedroom closet. Drawing is something I learned to do well and really enjoyed, but I haven't continued doing it much as an adult. For some reason my interest hasn't been there.

Being a Basketball Statistician

Just as in junior high, one of my favorite roles as the varsity basketball team manager was to keep statistics on shots taken during the game, who took each shot, and from where on the court. I made notes on a diagram of a basketball court for each quarter so the coaches would know who took shots from where. I also kept the scoring for each player for each game. I tallied their performances and produced simple reports for the coaches showing each player's average score. I eventually kept track of this information for our whole conference – who the leading scorers were across all our teams – and this information was provided to the coaches of all the teams. I loved this role and performed it well. Statistics seemed to click for me.

Oral Roberts University Basketball Camp

The summer after my junior year, my parents payed for me to go to the Oral Roberts University (ORU) basketball camp in Tulsa, Oklahoma. It was a great camp with about 100 kids from across our region. I was surprised to learn that I was rooming with a tall kid who was an excellent basketball player. In time I learned that he was the best player at the entire camp. I learned a lot and enjoyed staying in the dorms at ORU.

My parents had an ulterior motive for sending me to the camp, and we all knew it. They wanted me to attend college at ORU. They wanted me to like the campus and fall in love with it. I enjoyed my time there, and I did apply to ORU. We waited and waited for my acceptance letter, but it never came. I wasn't accepted, likely due to my poor high school performance and grades.

I have one distinct basketball memory from my experience there. We were running a basketball drill called the three-on-two full-court drill. Three players would run and pass and dribble a basketball down the length of the court and try to score against two opposing players waiting at the basket. If the basket was made, the two defensive players would be joined by one other player in line on the sideline, and they would drive down to the other end of the court in the same way, trying to score against the two players who were waiting to defend that basket. Once you had attempted to score, you would get back in line on the sideline and wait for your turn to get back onto the court to rerun the drill. It was a great drill. One of the times that I was charging down the court with two others, I made a bad pass and we missed making a basket. I was so frustrated that I looked up at the ceiling in disgust and kept moving forward, only to fall three feet down from the basketball court to the floor below! I wasn't used to playing on a raised court, in this case at the Mabee Center, which was an elaborate building with a complex setup. The next thing I knew I was lying on the floor beneath the basketball court. I felt so embarrassed in front of my fellow teammates; I had made a bad pass and then fallen off the court. I was already feeling weaker than the other campers, and this only made me feel worse. I was a guy who loved basketball and served as a manager on our high school team, not a varsity player or star from across the nearby states like most attending the camp.

My First Car

I learned to drive in my parents' large, light-blue Ford station wagon. It was a big car and safe for a brand-new driver. A little later I also drove their royal-blue Plymouth Duster.

I bought my first car when I was a junior in high school, after earning enough income working at Denny's. I purchased my car for $175 from my Aunt Jane. It was a 1964 Dodge Dart, which was 10 years old by the time I bought it. It had a push-button transmission,

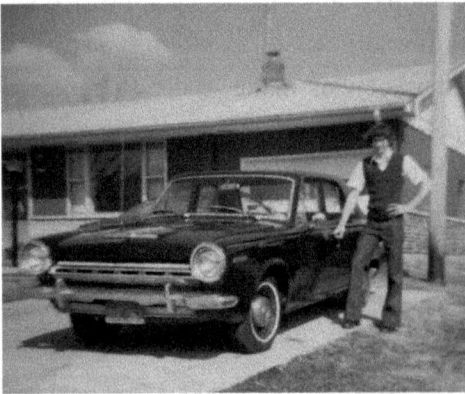

which is just what it sound like: you push a button to change gears and to reverse. It didn't have air conditioning other than rolling down your windows. I enhanced the car by installing an 8-track player in the glove compartment, and later I replaced it with a cassette deck in the same compartment so I could listen to my favorite music. I had that car for about two years, using it to commute to and from high school and work, and to visit my friends. I also drove it to and from college, just over two hours away. I eventually sold it for $250, after my first year away at college. I was able to use the car for three years and still made money on it. When I sold it I had significant trouble getting the driver's-side door to open. I often had to reach through the open window or press a quick "push and release" on the door button to get the door to open, but it was still a fine car. And I learned the basics of car ownership and how to maintain a vehicle: change the oil, replace a tire, change spark plugs, replace an air filter, replace the brakes, and so many other standard car maintenance activities. I have fond memories of my first car, my Dodge Dart.

New Covenant Fellowship

I grew up attending various Southern Baptist churches. During my high school years my parents developed a strong desire to deepen their relationships with God. They began attending a new charismatic church and various interdenominational prayer and worship services. I eventually joined them, attending services at New Covenant Fellowship in 1974. I attended the Sunday, Thursday night, and Saturday night services. It was a church I could relate to well.

We sang worship songs for almost an hour, with everyone in the building singing with expression in full voice, led by a band playing guitars, drums, brass, flute, and piano. Many of the lyrics were directly from scripture. New songs surfaced regularly. The tone was worship, not routine. This was so different from my prior experiences of singing three to five songs at a service, out of the same 30 to 40 hymns, for many years.

The church building was called the Sheep Shed. It was a prefabricated metal building on a concrete slab. It was almost always packed, filled with about 2,000 worshippers dressed in everything from jeans and T-shirts to formal suits. The services seemed to appeal to nearly every age and station in life, and the teachings felt genuine and down to earth.

We would arrive at least 30 minutes early to get good seats near the front. The energy, excitement, and expectations for each service were high. It was the first time I had experienced a church like that, where people arrived very early for seats close to the front and in order to visit with others before the service started. For me this was a completely new church-service experience.

At New Covenant I began to truly seek and worship God, for the first time seeing Him as an active part of my life. I loved attending the Saturday night services and listening to the teaching of youth pastor Ron Tucker. I truly related to his messages. It was at this point in my experience that I fell in love with worshipping God. The worship leaders, Ron Tucker and Kent Henry, led over 1,500 teens and 20-somethings into a deep passion and love for God through singing worship songs. We sang many choruses, often directly from scripture, and the tendency was to sing them slowly and over and over again, the same chorus, giving me the ability to meditate on the words. This experience significantly enhanced my desire to worship God for the rest of my life. I had never experienced anything like it.

I attended New Covenant until I left for college. I dreaded leaving St. Louis because I would miss the Saturday night services. On occasion some friends would join me for the two-hour drive back to St. Louis so we could attend a Saturday night service.

New Covenant Fellowship changed my church, my spiritual experience, and my life. I still have great memories today of my time there in the mid-1970s.

The Chair

I remember getting really mad only two times in my life, the first time was when I was a junior in high school. (The second time was after I was married, working on the brakes of our car.) The first time occurred when I was in my health class with Coach Lowrey as our teacher. I walked up to his desk to hand in an assignment, and one of my neighborhood friends – at least I thought we had been friends, for years – decided it would be fun to push my three-ring binder off the shelf of my desk chair where I had left it. My notebook hit the floor, the three rings opened up, and my papers went flying and sliding all over the floor. I immediately walked back to my desk, yelled at him, calling out his last name in a thunderous voice, then reached over, picked up my desk chair, and shoved it right on top of him. Then I calmly lifted it back off of him, set it back down in its usual place, and slowly gathered my papers from the floor and stuffed them back into my three-ring binder. Later I had to go back through all of them and reorganize them.

This all happened in the middle of the class. The teacher knew me well because I was the manager for the varsity basketball team and he was the assistant coach. He didn't do or say a thing. He let it all happen. He knew that if I had taken that action, surely the other kid was truly at fault. Class went on as though nothing had happened. I was mad at that friend for a long time. From that point on we were not as close as we had been.

Another friend might have also been in that class; I wouldn't be surprised if he had been. That friend often suggested that the friend who knocked my notebook to the floor do other crazy things, and often he would do them. When the two of them were together, even my mom called them "Nitro" and "Glycerin." Together they could frequently be real trouble; things always seemed to explode for the bad.

Gym Class

Gym was always my favorite class. I loved my time playing basketball, softball, team handball, volleyball, football, and almost every other physical activity we were taught. I loved that class so much that I took three gym classes back to back during my last semester of my senior year. Rather than dressing out for gym and then changing back into my school clothes for each of my other classes, I only had to change once, and then I would enjoy my three gym classes back to back.

Our Senior Class Trip

With only about two weeks left in my high school experience, I traveled to St. Augustine and Daytona Beach, Florida, in a large air-conditioned bus with over 55 other kids for our week-long high school senior trip. I met many seniors for the first time; I really didn't know many kids in my own class. For some reason each year I seemed to be closest to kids from other grades, and often it would be the seniors of that year. They would then graduate and leave school, so the next year I had to make new friends. So I didn't develop close friends in high school. I was sociable with those I played basketball with, but we weren't really close friends. (I recently visited with several classmates at my 50-year high school reunion,

and it was great to see them after not having seen any of them in over 50 years.)

I think we had three chaperone teachers with us on the trip. My one close friend, Mike, to whom I grew closer during that last semester, encouraged me to join him on the trip. I'm so glad I did, as I had a real blast. We enjoyed spending time with many seniors I had never met. Some I had heard of because they were popular, but others I didn't know anything about. Mike was friends with a number of them and introduced me to them.

It was a fantastic trip and I met so many more people in my own grade. Some of us became so close that during the following summer I spent a lot of time visiting and playing with many of them. There was a good reason I hadn't known these kids until then: almost all of them were great students with excellent grades who took advanced-level classes. They knew each other, but not kids like me who took the easiest classes we could find and only cared about getting a C and passing. At one point on the Florida trip they were comparing their ranks in our grade: one was number three, another number five, another number seven, and so on. And that was out of just over 880 kids in our grade. I later looked up my rank and learned that I was in the top half of our class; I ranked about 440. It was fun to meet these great kids. I only wish I had met them much earlier in school.

The Last Day of School

I remember driving away from the parking lot after my last day of school in my dark-blue Dodge Dart. I turned left and up the road, celebrating the fact that I had completed my high school years and had no more homework, at least from that institution. I turned on my 8-track player and selected the Alice Cooper song "School's Out." One of the lines in the song says, "School's out forever!" I cranked up the music and was singing at the top of my lungs as I sped up the street. Suddenly I was rudely surprised by a red light at the intersection that I had just driven through. I was so caught up in celebrating the end of high school that I wasn't paying attention to the road. I was thankful I wasn't hit by a car at this small intersection, but it shocked me to realize that I could have been killed in a car accident only minutes after graduating from high school! I was still pleased about my graduation, but after my life flashed before my eyes I turned down the music and started paying much closer attention to the road I was traveling on as I drove home.

Graduation Summer

The summer after graduation was so fun. No school, just my part-time job at McDonald's, leaving me with plenty of free time and some spending money. I spent a lot of time playing basketball or tennis with either my friend Kevin and some of his friends or with Mike. Mike and I also spent a lot of time visiting and playing games, sometimes swimming at a pool, going to a movie, attending a concert, and so many other activities with my new friends Barb, Megan, Donna, Diane, Cathy, and Darlene, and a few others on occasion. Mike and I

spent so many hours with these girls. We had an interest in some of them, but we were first and foremost just good friends who enjoyed spending time together and laughing. No romantic relationships. We visited each other's homes, played games, TPed houses at night, and enjoyed each other's company. There were times when I wondered how this was happening; I had never spent any time with girls, and now that was mostly how I spent my time, along with Mike.

Since that summer I haven't had much contact with any of them, but it sure was a fun summer. One of the things we enjoyed most was toilet-papering friends' houses at night. We would buy several rolls, go to a friend's address, and fling a roll of toilet paper high into the air, spinning it as it flew so that a long string of toilet paper would unroll and hang from the limbs of a tree. We would continue this process until the roll was used up, then grab another roll and repeat. Our goal was to decorate their yard with as many toilet paper strands as possible, hanging from as many trees as we could manage. I'm sure it was a mess to clean up, but to us it was a thing of beauty to see a yard full of dangling toilet paper. We hit one tree-filled yard with over 50 rolls of toilet paper.

One time Mike and I were planning an assault on a friend's house. We had just stopped at a store and loaded my trunk with TP rolls. As we planned our next move, a police car pulled into the parking lot and walked over to us. He wanted us to open our trunk. Surely he was looking for drugs or guns or something like that, but all he found was a trunk loaded with toilet paper rolls. I think he had a good idea what we were up to, but he didn't require anything of us other than to stay out of trouble. We were caught, but not in the act.

Once I was training my cousin Kirk how to TP a house, and a police car came down the street, so we all hid in the bushes in front of the various homes. Kirk wasn't experienced at this, so as soon as the police car drove away he started walking out of the bushes, only to see that the police car had turned around and was coming right back down the street. The policeman put a spotlight on him and called him over to the car. To our disadvantage, Kirk called out our names and pointed to where we were. We received a slight reprimand, but I don't remember anything else happening.

Decorating a house with toilet paper rolls was a lot of fun for several of us – friends from school and some from McDonald's. It may have destroyed the look of a yard for a short time, but at least it wasn't long-term damage to someone's property.

High School Experience Assessment

One morning in 2024 I reflected on my high school experience. We had recently attended Carolyn's 50-year high school reunion. I pulled out my 1975 yearbook, which prompted many thoughts about that period in my life almost a half century earlier. I looked through the group activities and senior photos sections, but I wasn't in even one photo. There were at least 35 highlighted groups including sports, clubs, and events; I was not a part of any of them. During my first two or three years of high school I was a basketball team manager, but by my senior year I had no involvement with any groups until our senior trip to Florida. My whole goal was to get through high school without getting into trouble or being noticed. I took almost no advantage of the educational and relational experiences available to me. In fact I utilized very little from those 12 years of formal education in developing myself. I had no idea how my education would relate to my future. None. I wanted out, to be in the real world, to be on my own, to play and enjoy the life I had.

During high school I felt like I was different from everyone else, but looking back, I was probably like many, if not most, of my classmates. I was a loner trying to just get through or by. I felt like I couldn't relate to or be involved with others because I wasn't smart and because of my Christian beliefs and habits. I didn't cuss, drink, smoke, or interact with girls. I played sports – mainly basketball – and that was about it.

I lost so much by neglecting my personal development, failing to capitalize on learning opportunities, and not nurturing my relational skills and friendships. I pretty much threw so much of those 12 years of my life away while my peers were moving ahead, learning upon learning, developing upon developing. I wasted my life's jump-start. It was like sitting at the starting line of a 50-yard dash while those around me were sprinting for the first 20 yards, at which point I would finally stand and start to jog toward the finish line, knowing that if I didn't finish the race I would be in trouble with my parents. I would cross the line – probably last – but I would meet the school's minimum requirements and my parents' expectations.

It's heartbreaking now to reflect on all the opportunities that were right in front of me that I didn't seize. Whoever you are, your education really matters. I hope my younger readers will take this very seriously. Each thing you learn opens the door to additional learning opportunities. Please take advantage of as many opportunities as you can as early as you can, because it will make a tremendous difference for your future. Hopefully you won't have to play as much catch-up as I have over the past 50 years or so.

Chapter 7

Favorite Family Trips

My parents took us on many vacations, lasting at least a week or two. We almost always camped, regardless of the weather. Most of these were while I was in grade school.

Elephant Rocks

I think my parents took us to Elephant Rocks State Park in Missouri multiple times. I loved climbing up the immense, pink, rounded rocks. I enjoyed climbing up a rock and then transferring to another massive rock, repeating the process over and over.

Johnson's Shut-Ins

I also loved playing in the water and on the rocks of Johnson's Shut-Ins State Park. Once when we were visiting, my dad had to jump into the water to save Colleen from drowning in one of the deep pools with whirling water that can pull you down under the surface. He tossed his camera to my mom and then dove in after her.

My own kids had a similar experience, likely in the same place, when Carolyn had to dive in to save Tim and Michelle, who were both struggling to stay afloat because of the water sucking them down into a pool. She was able to save both of them.

Williamsburg and Jamestown

I remember falling in love with Colonial Williamsburg, Virginia, particularly the tricornered hats, flintlock pistols and rifles, and learning about our American history. I also enjoyed visiting the Jamestown settlement just a few miles away.

New York World's Fair

We visited New York and went to the New York World's Fair in 1964. The admission price for an adult was $2.00. There were so many special displays, including the Unisphere, the central and most iconic feature – a giant stainless-steel globe symbolizing the fair's theme. It's a Small World, a popular ride featuring animatronic children from around the world, was created by Walt Disney. It later appeared in many Disney theme parks. Carousel of Progress, another Disney attraction, featured a rotating theater showcasing life in different eras and highlighting technological changes through animatronics. Futurama II, General Motors' exhibit, offered imaginative views of future societies and cities. The Uniroyal Tire was a giant 80-foot Ferris wheel shaped like a tire, featuring a polyester resin and fiberglass shell, 24 gondolas, and a 100-horsepower motor. It was a moving advertisement for the company's products, with the gondolas' seats made of Naugahyde and the floors carpeted with a Uniroyal nylon product.

Coney Island

My parents took us to Coney Island, which is a historic neighborhood and amusement area in South Brooklyn, New York, famous for its boardwalk, beach, and iconic attractions. I remember the parachute-jump ride that took riders high into the air and let them float down with a parachute. The parachute was connected with cables to ensure riders would float directly down to the bottom. That ride closed in September of 1964, just after we were there.

Statue of Liberty

We were able to see the Statue of Liberty and climb to its crown. The climb involves 162 narrow, tight, spiral steps – the only way to get to the top – and visitors must be able to navigate them without significant physical or mental issues.

Disneyland

My parents drove us all the way to California from St. Louis for a vacation. The drive was over 1,800 miles and took over 30 hours. We saw many sights along the way, and Disneyland was one of the main attractions we enjoyed. We rode on the Matterhorn Bobsleds, which opened in 1959; it was the world's first tubular steel roller coaster and a popular thrill ride.

Yellowstone

We went to Yellowstone National Park and enjoyed watching Old Faithful, one of the world's best-known geysers, as it erupted high into the air. I also remember the terrible smell of many of the geothermal pools.

Jean Talon in Montreal, Canada

My dad drove our family all around Montreal, Canada, looking for the Montreal Expos' stadium on Jean Talon Street. We kept asking locals for help finding it, and they kept saying another name – the name as you would say it in French. We were mispronouncing it, which caused a lot of confusion when we tried to get help. We eventually found it, and I was able to see the baseball park that the Montreal Expos major league baseball team used at the time.

The Grand Canyon

Our parents took us to see the immense Grand Canyon in northern Arizona. I don't remember many details, but I do remember being impressed and awed by the view.

Carolyn and I also took our kids to the Grand Canyon and had a great time. (I share more about our Independence Day experience at the north rim of the Grand Canyon in the next *Grampy, Grampy* book about my adult experiences.)

Devil's Tower

We also went to Devil's Tower National Monument in Wyoming. The rock tower is an astounding geologic feature that protrudes out of the prairie surrounding the Black Hills. It's a unique natural structure. It looks like claws have scraped downward on the giant rock formation from a very tall height. It's considered sacred by Northern Plains Indians and other indigenous peoples. Hundreds of parallel cracks make it one of the finest crack-climbing areas in North America.

Garden of the Gods

We enjoyed many special places in Colorado, including the huge red rock formations called Garden of the Gods. It was like a much larger version of the Elephant Rocks park in Missouri that I enjoyed so much. (In my next book I'll describe visiting a park that makes Garden of the Gods look small: Arches National Park in Utah, which has become one of my favorite places on this planet. I didn't visit Arches as a kid, but I have many times as an adult.)

We also visited Seven Falls, and Pike's Peak, which is a 14,115-foot mountain near Colorado Springs, Colorado. I fell in love with Colorado. I even produced a book report about it in grade school.

Mount Rushmore

We went to Mount Rushmore National Memorial, which is a massive sculpture carved into Mount Rushmore in the Black Hills region of South Dakota. It was completed in 1941. The sculpture's roughly 60-foot-high granite faces depict U.S. presidents George Washington, Thomas Jefferson, Theodore Roosevelt, and Abraham Lincoln. It was impressive!

More Vacation Trips

My parents took us on many other trips including to Florida; Albuquerque, New Mexico; and eastern Canada. We almost always camped in a tent or a tent trailer that we pulled behind our car. It opened up with two sides sliding outward to create an above-ground tent for our family of five to sleep in. My dad even installed portable cots that doubled as bunk beds, allowing us to sleep above and below.

Vacations were when I could spend more time with my dad and our whole family. While I was growing up my dad spent many evenings attending college classes, studying for classes, building something, or working on a major project such as adding a carport to the side of our house, converting it to a garage, building a bathroom, building my room in the basement, and adding a full family room to the back of the house. He was a very busy guy.

Now it's time to learn a little about how Carolyn grew up.

Chapter 8

Grandma: Carolyn May Warnky

I was born Carolyn May Beukema in Panama City, Panama, in 1958. My parents were missionaries with the World Radio Missionary Fellowship. (This is now known as HCJB Global — HCJB being the call letters of the missionary radio station.) Over the years they served in Panama and in Quito, Ecuador, with some stints in the U.S. also. I was the youngest of five children, with two sisters and two brothers. Most of the interactions I remember from my childhood were with my brother Steve, who is three-and-a-half years older than I am. My other siblings are six to nine years older, so we didn't do a lot together.

Panama

My growing-up years were not as independent as Grampy's. In Panama we lived in the center of a big city, right across the main street from the Canal Zone. We kids attended school in the Zone, which was in English and very similar to American schools. My brother Ron graduated from high school there, but my last school year in Panama was second grade.

Most of the time we lived in a two-bedroom apartment that was close to the radio station where my parents worked. There was a divider in the dining room with bunk beds on one side for my two brothers. My sisters and I shared a bedroom. I remember stories of them getting in trouble for giggling together when they should have been sleeping.

The building had stores on the first floor and apartments on the second and third floors facing the street. In the back there was a tiled patio area over the back half of the stores. This served the apartments as a place to hang laundry and for kids to play. I remember roller-skating across the tiles with the metal wheels going "ka-chunk, ka-chunk." Back then roller skates clamped onto your feet over your shoes. You had a tool that was called a key that you used to loosen and tighten the skates. My siblings and I probably shared skates, since we could adjust the size.

One highlight of our week was going to the library in the Canal Zone. It was air-conditioned, which we didn't always have in our apartment. Most of the time we lived there we didn't have a TV. There isn't much evening daylight in the tropics because the sun sets at about 6:00 PM all year long. We all did a lot of reading in the evening for relaxation.

Driving through Central America

We drove through Central America three times, once from Panama to Michigan and twice from Michigan to Panama. We had a three-row station wagon and pulled a tent trailer to sleep in. On at least one of the trips Ron slept in the back of the station wagon. On the last trip there were only five of us because Ron and my sister Sue stayed in the Chicago area to continue their education. The northbound trip was when the whole family moved to the U.S. after Ron's high school graduation.

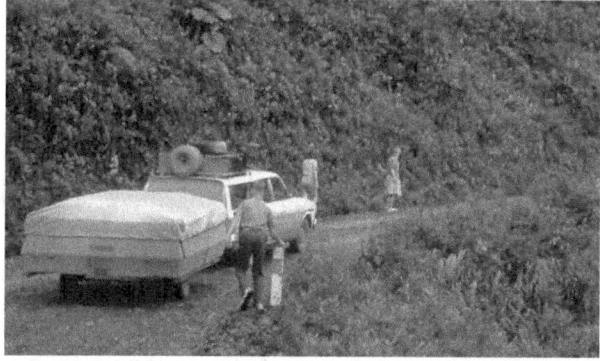

Michigan

While I was in third and fourth grade, we lived near Grand Rapids, Michigan, for about two years. Our house was more like the typical houses in the suburbs of that time than the apartment we had in Panama. I learned how to ride a bike, and we had a TV. I remember watching *Bewitched*, *I Dream of Jeannie*, and *Hogan's Heroes*. I had a generic doll, a Barbie imitation, and my mom and I would make clothes for it. I remember snow sledding down a big hill we had in the backyard.

Both of my parents were from Michigan, so much of our extended family lived there and I had opportunities to play with many of my cousins in Big Rapids, Michigan. We were also able to spend holiday times with my dad's family in the Grand Rapids area.

Quito, Ecuador

After my fourth grade, my parents went back to the mission field, this time in Quito, Ecuador. Anita, Steve, and I were still living at home, so we three siblings and my parents drove south to Panama and then flew to Quito. Ecuador is a country in South America that straddles the equator. Quito is a beautiful city in a valley in the Andes mountains at an elevation of about 9,350 feet. Even though Ecuador is in the tropics, Quito doesn't have hot temperatures because of its altitude. The weather is more like what we call spring. Every year there are rainy and dry seasons, but no fall or winter. There is a jungle nearby in the Amazon Basin and a coastal area along the Pacific Ocean.

Our first residence in Ecuador was an apartment on the mission compound where the studio and office buildings housed the radio ministry. The mission operated AM and FM stations and a shortwave

station that broadcast worldwide in many languages.

The school we attended was just down the block, and it was a private school called the Alliance Academy. It was run by the Christian and

Missionary Alliance to provide American-style education for the children of missionaries. There were also students whose parents were diplomats or worked for American companies. We had Bible classes and Spanish classes every day, but the rest of the curriculum was like any American school, although more rigorous than many. The elementary grades, a dorm, and the sports field were in a walled compound on one side of the street. The junior and senior high classrooms, along with the gymnasium, were on the other side of the street. There were a handful of dorms in the city for children of missionaries working in other South American countries or in different parts of Ecuador, such as the jungle.

I have many fond memories of Quito. I had a good friend, Allyson, who lived in the apartment below ours, which made the transition easier for me. It was harder for Anita because she was in high school and didn't have all the credits she would need to graduate. She ended up going back to Michigan halfway through her senior year and living with my grandparents so she could graduate there.

Because I was older than I had been in Panama, I had more independence. We lived in many different places, but most of them were within walking distance of the school and the mission compound. I could usually walk to my friends' homes, and as my friends and I got older we could take city buses to stores.

I lived in Quito for six years. My first school year was a combination of fifth and sixth grades. (The school suggested to my parents that I skip from fifth to sixth grade partway through the year because of my academic abilities and because I was tall and mature for my age.) The next three years, my seventh through ninth grades, were in the same school. After living in the States again for two years, my last year of high school was also at the Alliance Academy. And I went back to Quito as a "working visitor" at HCJB for most of a year during my university time in the States.

During elementary school I set a trend during recess of reading while roller-skating! I had to have good peripheral vision to read a book and skate by other kids without running into anyone.

There wasn't much opportunity for competitive sports for girls at that time, but many of us wanted to be cheerleaders. As I was going into junior high school (seventh and eighth grades), that was my goal. Allyson had an older sister who was a varsity cheerleader, so we practiced what we learned from her in their backyard. We had to try out at a pep rally in front of the whole junior and senior high grades. I didn't make the squad during my first tryout, but I was a cheerleader in eighth and ninth grades and then again in my last year. Cheerleading was not part of their culture, so our school was unusual in that regard.

The Alliance had one of the nicest gyms in the city at that time, so the boys' basketball team played many games, sometimes even against military schools. I knew of only one other English-speaking school in the city, so most of the games were against Ecuadorians. Our school played some soccer, but there weren't many games. Our field was small and our team was probably much worse than the local teams since South Americans grow up playing soccer.

We attended an English-speaking church and participated in various activities through the church and the school. Although I had Spanish classes every year, I was never really immersed in Spanish, so I didn't become very fluent. All my friends spoke English, and we spoke English at home. Other families were more assimilated into the Ecuadorian culture. Allyson's family attended a Spanish-speaking church, and they were all very proficient in the language. Another friend, Christina, spoke German, Portuguese, Spanish, and English.

The school population was very transitory. During the summer months the dorm students would go back to their parents. A portion of the other students would leave the country to return home for furlough or to visit family. In different years I hung out with different friends.

I continued to read a lot, and my siblings and friends and I played a lot of games like Yahtzee and Rook. My parents believed that we shouldn't play with face cards (what most people think of as regular playing cards), dance, or go to movies. Movies and TV shows were in Spanish, so even if we had had a TV they wouldn't have appealed to me anyway. I didn't really feel deprived because I had my friends and books. At some point I learned to sew and made some of my own clothes. There was a public pool in the next valley, and sometimes a friend would take us there to swim. During the summer months I spent most of my time hanging out with my brother Steve and his friends. We would go to the coast for a week at a Christian camp. My family also took a few beach vacations during that time.

San Francisco, California

After Steve graduated from high school and I finished ninth grade, my parents took a leave of absence from the mission and we moved to the San Francisco area of California. I attended a public high school for my sophomore year and discovered that I had more class credits than was normal for a sophomore. Someone suggested that I could graduate from high school after attending for three years instead of four years if I wanted to. It was a lonely year for me because I was the only child still at home and I felt like an oddball at school. We attended a good church, but it wasn't close, so I didn't get together with people from church. My friend Ann, who was still in Quito, would mail me the school newsletter with handwritten notes about life at school there.

Back in Quito

Then my parents decided to return to the mission, and we moved back to Quito at the end of my sophomore school year. When I was

selecting classes for my junior year, I discovered that I was out of synch with the class progressions at the Alliance. Because it was a small school, elective classes were only offered at certain times; I would end up in my senior year with very few classes available. Then I remembered the suggestion to graduate in three years and decided to plan for it. I needed one correspondence course to meet my English requirement of four years, but everything else worked out well. So I started my last year as a junior, even getting elected to the Student Council, and ended the year as a senior. (My friend Christina and another friend also finished in three years.)

During that last school year my brother Ron and his family moved to Ecuador for several months so Ron could work on his doctoral field research in linguistics. He and his wife, Marj, and their two children, Kristi and Peter, lived in a town high in the mountains where Ron studied the Quichua language. My Grandma Beukema also came to visit us that year for a few weeks. I wasn't sure what I was going to do after graduation, and she convinced me to go back to the States for college, even though I would be only sixteen.

Greenville College

I attended Greenville College in Greenville, Illinois, in the fall of 1974. Greenville is relatively close to where my family lives in Michigan, and the college offered me scholarship money because my parents were missionaries. There were a few other students there from Ecuador, and I quickly made new friends. I was even a cheerleader in my freshman year.

Southern Illinois University

In 1976 I transferred to Southern Illinois University at Edwardsville (SIUE) to major in electrical engineering. Between my junior and senior years I visited my parents in Quito and ended up staying there for the school year and working in the station's engineering department. This gave me real-world work experience and allowed me to regroup after leaving home so young.

When I returned to SIUE for my senior year I discovered another good reason for being away for a year: By that time Chris Warnky had transferred to SIUE, and we met in a Christian Student Fellowship group. After two months we were engaged, and three months later we were married on the day after graduation.

Chapter 9

Conclusion

Thank You

Thank you for taking the time to read *Grampy, Grampy and Grandma...*, about these two fascinating journeys in the 1960s and 1970s. I hope you both enjoyed and learned something from our experiences. If you would like others to enjoy this sampling of life-experience as well, please leave a review at Amazon.com.

Learn More

Contact Information

Chris Warnky, author
   Cell phone: 614.787.8591 (call or text)
   Email: chriswarnky@gmail.com
   Facebook: welldonelife
   Website: chriswarnky.com
   Blog: http://cwarnky.wordpress.com

Thirteen percent of initial profits from sales of Chris's books is donated to Mission Aviation Fellowship (MAF), and subsequent profits to MAF and additional charities.

Acknowledgments

I'm thankful to our awesome Creator/God for allowing me to live my first 68 years and for providing me with many great relationships and experiences. I'm also thankful to have peace with Him because of the life and sacrifice of His Son, Jesus.

Thanks to my wife, Carolyn, for your love and especially for your support while I have been writing, editing, and publishing this and other books. I can't imagine going through anything without you by my side to celebrate our successes and support me in my times of failure and disappointment. I love you!

There are so many others I'm thankful to because of their contributions to my life. Below are a few of them:

Thanks to my mom and dad for all the love and support you have provided throughout my life. Thanks to Tim and Bonnie for your love and support. Thanks to Michelle and Joel for continually supporting me during my journey.

Thanks to Gwen Hoffnagle, my professional editor. You continue to take my original manuscripts to new heights. I enjoy working with you and appreciate the value you provide.

About the Author

Chris Warnky is 68 and has been married to Carolyn May Warnky for over 46 years. They have two children: Tim, who lives in Cleveland with his wife, Bonnie, and two daughters, Hannah and Lydia; and Michelle, who lives in Willard, Ohio, with her husband, Joel, and daughter, Grace, and is a popular multiyear *ANW* competitor and a serious, competitive obstacle-course racer.

Chris is an active, training ninja warrior. He competed in the 2017 *ANW Cleveland City Qualifiers.* His awe and wonder of God is the basis of his life. He is the author of 13 books, with several more in progress.

www.ingramcontent.com/pod-product-compliance
Lightning Source LLC
Chambersburg PA
CBHW061744020426
42331CB00006B/1349